Teen-Age Glamor

Teen-Age Glamor

ADAH BROADBENT

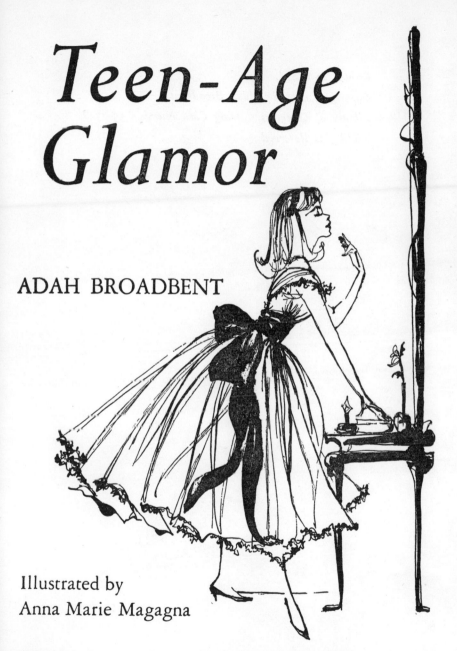

Illustrated by
Anna Marie Magagna

DOUBLEDAY & COMPANY, INC., GARDEN CITY, NEW YORK

*This book
is dedicated in loving memory
to my parents*

Contents

Teen-Age Glamor

COLOR MAGIC

Colors are the beauty and the magic which create
exciting miracles. Color harmonies are as delicate as
frosty lace on a windowpane, as powerful as Wagner's
music, as monotonous as the slap of little waves on a
sandy beach, or as brilliant as the splendor of Roman
candles against the velvet darkness. At times you catch
your breath at the loveliness of color.

Don't you remember some of the times when color

has increased your pleasure in a favorite sweater, a smart hat, and a flattering scarf? No doubt you recall many other impressions of color.

Some colors you like better than others. What are your favorite colors and what do they do for you? Color creates your mood—raising your spirit or depressing it, chilling or warming your heart, giving your mind excitement or serenity. There are colors which sing a happy tune, colors which are a requiem; some which emphasize, those which camouflage; some approach and others retreat. This chapter tells you which colors have these different qualities.

Many an artist spends his life experimenting with color and delights in using it with distinction. Often certain artists are associated with certain colors. Here are three artists, Titian, Van Gogh, and Gauguin, who are famous for their exceptionally beautiful color harmonies.

Titian lived about five hundred years ago in the beautiful city of Venice, the Jewel of the Adriatic. The pomp and splendor of Venice are reflected in Titian's magnificent colors, which seem to glow with richness and depth. You want to touch—to feel them. Perhaps this is the reason Titian admired and painted women with red hair, the color of copper with gleaming highlights and mysterious shadows. This is "Titian red" and is recalled with delight. If your hair has these tones, choose your colors from Titian's masterpieces. Whether you can wear these colors or not, you can admire and enjoy Titian's genius with his rich, sumptuous colors.

Another artist, Van Gogh, created unusual and beautiful color harmonies. Leaving his native Holland with the penetrating chill of fog and the sharp cutting wind from gray skies, he went to the south of France and there discovered the hot blazing sun. He keyed his colors to the brilliant sunshine, and "Van Gogh green" is the green of hills and fields drenched in the liquid gold of the sunshine he loved so well. These sharp vivid colors may be for you, try them.

A French artist, Gauguin, who lived about fifty years ago, was a friend of Van Gogh's. Gauguin, too, painted the sunshine, but not with Van Gogh's intensity. Living in the South Sea Islands, Gauguin painted the hot, heavy quietness of the tropics. Gauguin magnificently designed his masterpieces with stylized —yet expressive—figures and broad masses of color. The warm exotic "Gauguin pink" is a superb contrast to the dark-green leaves and purple shadows which are motionless in the heat. You girls with black hair and olive skins will happily realize these sultry colors are among those which you can wear. Everyone can enjoy Gauguin's extraordinary color harmonies.

Dior, the French fashion authority, creates his masterpieces in the world of clothes with a sensitive feeling for line and color which establishes him as an artist. His exceptionally fine color sense combines sea green with Madonna blue, which is refreshingly modern and as timelessly beautiful as a Botticelli painting. Is it surprising that Dior is famous for his color harmonies?

The choice of colors tells us about the temperament of an artist. Remember that all paintings have something for you.

Color has always been important, it plays an impressive part in the ceremonial rituals of every civilization. Through the centuries there has developed a symbolism of color in the Church. In the paintings of the Madonna and Child by the Old Masters the Virgin's robe is always blue; this lovely, serene color is an inseparable part of her.

Always, color is an integral part of a land and its culture. Think of the mellow tones of ancient marble against the intense blue of Grecian skies, and the splendor of pink, vermilion, gold, and purple of India, the land of contrasts and drama.

Perhaps the reason we feel no restraint in the use and choice of color is because people from everywhere are part of our country. Our arts result from the combination of old cultures with the vigorous aggressiveness of pioneers. Here color is investigated scientifically, as well as aesthetically, and innumerable uses are found for it.

Among the artist-designers who realize a knowledge of color is essential are:

interior decorators
architects
landscape architects
milliners
designers of:

jewelry	furniture
shoes	stage sets
textiles	clothing
wallpaper	books and magazines

The complete list is longer.

Designers, top-flight in their fields, use color subtly and expertly. Most people, having no knowledge of the artists' brilliant creativeness, respond only to the magic which the artists have wrought.

Color sets the mood of a play, points up the action, and emphasizes the importance of certain actors. For instance, on the stage the deep, tragic loneliness of Hamlet is keenly felt. Would the emotional impact be the same if the stage settings were painted in gaily singing colors? Absurd! Those colors belong to a chorus line of can-can dancers. Which colors would *you* use in staging "The Snow Queen"?

Learn enough about color to recognize and appreciate the genius of Jo Mielziner, who designed the stage settings for *The King and I,* and the remarkable talents of Mme. Karinska, who created the mermaid costumes for *Hans Christian Andersen.*

Every day in a thousand ways, you react to color—discover all you can about it. Where to start? Why not with nature? Look for exquisite and intriguing color harmonies *everywhere.* The sunsets, the tones of green on a hillside, the subtle range of colors in a lake, the dark trees silhouetted against a cloudy sky, the sun pouring flaming heat on a cornfield. There is no limit to the beauty, the delicacy, the magnificence of nature's color rhythms. These are all part of your life, look for them.

To broaden your conception further, here are some fundamentals which are important to your understanding and to your handling of color. First, the color wheel!

Artists arrange colors in a circle called the color wheel, with the lightest color, yellow, at the top; the other two primaries, red and blue, are placed on the left and right sides. When two primaries are combined in equal amounts the result is a secondary color. The secondaries are orange, green, and purple. Place green between yellow and blue, orange between red and yellow, and purple between red and blue. Mixing a primary and an adjacent secondary, you have the colors red-orange, yellow-orange, blue-green, yellow-green, red-violet, and blue-violet. These are called tertiaries. Do you recognize some of these tertiary colors by the trade names of scarlet (red-orange), chartreuse (yellow-green), turquoise (blue-green), fuchsia (red-violet), and shocking pink (tint of red-violet)? Why not take some colored paper or crayons or water colors and make your own color wheel? You will discover thousands of tints and shades. If you like to cut and paste, buy colored paper at a stationery or art store. It is easy to make a color wheel.

Dyes, paints, inks are grayed (neutralized) because pure colors are too raw, too brilliant to be used. How is a color grayed? Mix it with the complement, the complement being the color across from it on the color wheel. The complement of yellow is purple, the com-

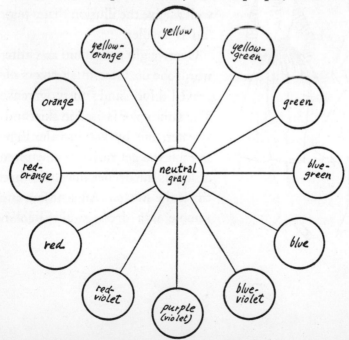

plement of red is green, and the complement of blue is orange. The complement of the tertiary yellow-green is red-violet, the complement of yellow-orange is blue-violet, and the complement of red-orange is blue-green.

This neutralizing may be so slight that the uninformed eye only realizes that the color is *pleasingly* bright, not glaringly brilliant, or this neutralization can continue until the result is a grayed misty hue and if further mixing is done a neutral gray emerges.

These grayed, hazy colors play an important role. The American artist, Whistler, used them exclusively and labeled his masterpieces with such titles as "Symphony in White" and "Nocturne: Blue and Silver."

These muted colors are ideally suited for clothes because they flatter many complexions and eyes as well as give the illusion that a person is smaller.

Overweight girls build an entire wardrobe on these quiet colors of grayed blues and misty greens. The same color is used in skirt and sweater, but by varying the tone in each you get variety; sometimes a skirt is the deeper hue and other times the sweater. A becoming ensemble is a dress in the lighter tones of Scottish heather and a cardigan sweater two tones darker. Plump girls never break the color by adding a differently colored belt, scarf, collar, cuffs, or hat. Many a downfall is caused by the white blouse and dark skirt, which takes inches from the height and adds them to the width. Be "one color" from hemline to hat. This is technically called a monochromatic color scheme; "mono" means one and "chromatic" is color. This unbroken color always slenderizes and heightens.

Girls who are short-waisted or short-legged should wear blouse, sweater or jacket, and skirt the same color and tone. Be a monochromatic color harmony. The reverse is true for the tall slender girl, who breaks color by having blouse, skirt, and belt all different hues—if she likes.

Another rule of color which deals with complements is the "intensifying of a color by its complement." A simpler way to say it is—when complements are near each other, both colors are stronger. Yellow and purple are complements; therefore when a complexion tends to be sallow avoid all purple hues, because the purple emphasizes the yellowish skin tone; however, if you are a blonde the lilac and fuchsia tones accentuate your yellow hair. Ruddy complexions avoid the "green family," the aquas, the turquoises, chartreuses, emerald greens, or faces become very red. The greens and blue-greens accentuate the vivid highlights of red hair. The dash, the zing, of complementary color harmonies is perfect for girls with vivid personalities.

Seurat was an artist who used complementary colors to attain scintillating effects on his canvases. In the Art Institute of Chicago, Seurat's famous painting, "A Summer Sunday on the Grande Jatte," is composed of thousands and thousands of bits of pure paint; red and green, yellow and purple, blue and orange. Each complement vibrates with the other, producing a truly luminous effect.

Another interesting law of color is the "one color predominates." In a work of art, be it picture, a mural or a dress, one color is used more than any other. This principal color may be subdued, contrasted, or emphasized with a touch of vivid or contrasting color which balances the larger area of dominating color. Perhaps beads, scarf, hat, or flowers strike the contrasting highlights with your dominant color. If your dark-green suit is faded or too dull in color, pin red carnations on your lapel and watch the green brighten. On the other hand, a corsage of daffodils subdues the same green hue. The chapter "Precious Little" tells you more about color in accessories. In fact, you will find the laws of color and line throughout the book.

In glancing again at the color wheel, those hues on the left are called the "warm colors"; red, yellow,

orange, and all their tints and shades are those seen in
flames of fire. The characteristics of this group are
dominating, exciting, aggressive, gay, and happy. An
essential principle for you to remember is that these
colors apparently *increase* the size of an object—optical
illusion. The conclusion is—big hips avoid skirts in red,
gold, scarlet, burgundy, orange, and other warm colors.
Your sweater has generous curves? Avoid the "fire
colors."

On the right side of the color wheel are the cool
colors, the blues and violets which are found in the
shadows of ice and snow, in the cool depths of a lake.
The myriad hues of blue, blue-green, blue-violet, and
purple are cool, calm, serene, and dignified. The
formality and beauty of purple make it a royal color.

The cool tones are better in the large areas; the ex-
panses of sky, grass, and ocean are from this group.
Overweight girls select cool colors because these hues
minimize the size of any object as do the darker shades.
The darker the suit, the smaller you apparently are;
a navy suit slenderizes you more than a gray one does.
The reverse is true, the tints (light tones), the pastels
increase your size.

In spite of the very obvious laws of color there are
some remarkably wrong statements made about the
wearing of colors. Many say, "Gold is perfect for

brunettes." There are thousands of brunettes with subtly different coloring and hundreds of tones of gold. Some are flattering and some are not. Another fallacy is, "Brunettes can't wear blue." It just isn't true. It is said, "Never wear green and red together." Of course you can! Many combinations of red and green are stunning. The Egyptians used these complementary colors often. Perfect together are a certain red and pink. All colors "go together" if they are the right value and tone. Look at sunsets. Did you ever see one with clashing colors?

The general rule, in choosing flattering colors to wear, is—match your skin tone. Those skins which have ocher or olive tints find the warm hues complimentary, while the complexions with pink and red undertones need the cool colors. Remember, this is the *general* rule and can often be ignored advantageously. Some of you should accentuate your hair or eyes rather than your skin.

Experimentation is the best way; truly, it is the *only sure way*. Collect lengths of fabric or rolls of crepe paper in every imaginable color: these lengths should be about a yard long. Your club could assemble this material and the cost would be small for each girl. Drape the material around your shoulders in the light in which you intend to wear it. Does it enhance your skin, emphasize the gleaming highlights of your hair, give luster to your eyes? If it doesn't, it isn't for you.

Ask yourself these same questions when you buy yard goods and clothes.

After watching hundreds of girls try these rainbows of colors, I discovered that a bright navy blue clears and lightens most complexions. Every color changes the color of your skin tones in some way. Investigate your color possibilities.

When eyes are your best feature, emphasize them with color. Mary, who has the most gorgeous gray eyes, which are sometimes seen in those with a strain of Welsh blood, has a smoky gray chiffon evening dress, the circular skirt splashed with vivid poppies. She is utterly enchanting. Cynthia's blue eyes are as blue as cornflowers when she wears her purple suit.

Red-haired girls are lucky. Never tone down that hair, be it flaming orange or rich glowing copper. Enhance it with color, flatter it with brushing until

the highlights gleam. Try all the colors, and you will be amazed at those you can and should wear. Start with the pinks, apricots, aquas, turquoises, peacock blues, lilacs, corals, and chartreuses in all their different tints and shades. You can wear tones of all of them. Kiki, who was born with copper-colored hair and a sure sophisticated color sense, discovered when very young an exquisite pink, which is "truly hers."

Sometimes gray, beige (sand), and brown subdue the highlights in brown hair, making it seem lifeless; discard these and wear those colors which flatter. Experiment with the "green family."

Fashion decrees each season's colors. Sometimes current events sway color choices. In the year of the English Coronation, all the fashion magazines wrote of Coronation colors. The fabulous colors of uniforms, dresses with regal trains, and jewels echoed in the highlights of the stained-glass windows in Westminster Abbey were universally used by dress designers and jewelers.

When *The King and I* opened in New York, the spectacular color combinations of Siam, the shocking pink, peacock blue, gold and cerise were featured, copied, and used by the leading fashion authorities. Watch for yourself what happens in style and colors the next time some unusual show is presented.

Certain colors synchronize with specific seasons.

Think of the harvest colors in the autumn: the red of winesap apples, the luscious purples of sun-ripened grapes, the scarlet maple trees touched with frost. In Indian summer, have you ever seen the copper leaves of beech trees against the deep blue of an October sky, the quiet browns of trees and ground when the first flakes of snow start to fall? These colors distinguish the palette of the dress designers in the autumn.

When icy blasts whip up a blizzard, the warm, rich, sumptuous colors, the burgundy reds, holly greens, the deep red of winter berries, the molten golds and the vibrant purples are a joy to see and to wear.

Spring gives us a wide choice of pastel colors, starting with the delicate greens of new leaves. These delightful colors along with others for hot weather are explained at length in the chapter "Summer Icicles."

This first chapter gives you the information about how to choose and enjoy color. Some of you hide a sparkling personality with drab, dull colors. Other girls wear brilliant colors which overpower their appearance and personality; remember, the demure jenny wren is as charming as the flamboyant parrot!

Discover beautiful and fascinating color harmonies for *you;* have a mind of your own and express your individuality. The "right" colors improve your appearance and give you a zest and sparkle. Remember, "Color creates your mood!"

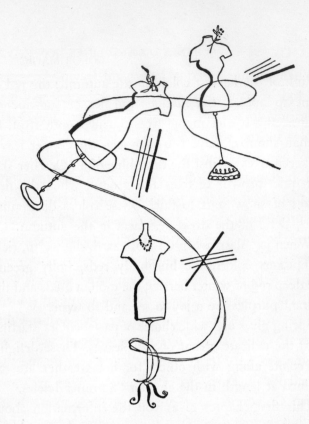

LINES DO AND LINES DON'T

There are lines which make you happy and lines which make you "blue." The Greeks called it "using optical illusion" for their statues and temples; I call it the "illusion of good proportion" for teen-agers, because the lines of your clothes can add to or subtract from your height, your weight, and your proportions.

When two lines of equal length are drawn ═══════
and four short diagonals are added >═══════< , it is
surprising to see one line appear longer. These rec-
tangles are the same size ▭ ▭ ▭ . Now watch
them change as by magic ▥ ▨ ▤ . By using vertical, horizontal, and diagonal lines the talented dress
designers create clothes which give the illusion of pleas-
ing proportions and correct weight to their clients'
figures. Because many of the top-flight designers are in
Hollywood, anyone, by going to the movies, can see
how cleverly the actresses are improved and glamor-
ized. The figure problems of the stars are rarely noticeable because the best features are emphasized and the
faults are camouflaged. In fact, one of the greatest dress
designers enlisted in the Camouflage Corps during the
Second World War.

Joan Crawford, a well-dressed actress, wears floor-
length evening dresses with sweeping vertical lines
to give her the longer-legged look which she prefers.

There are other famous actresses who have short
necks, long arms, or short waists, and so on ad infi-
nitum. Acting is an enormously competitive business
and actresses must do something about their problems,
no wishful thinking for them!

When you go to a movie, study the figure proportions of any actress. Can you discover her figure problem and how it is camouflaged? By color and line! If

the actress is small above the waist, her blouse is a warm color and her height is increased by vertical lines. Many many more examples can be given. You soon realize that there is more here than meets the eye; study and analyze. The movies can tell you many things besides a good story.

Do you have any figure problems? Are you satisfied with your proportions and only want more flattering clothes, or is a change of bodily proportions indicated? Whatever your conclusion, this book will help you develop your talents to be an artist-designer.

First, simplicity is the fundamental truth behind the smart, smooth look. No matter what your size or shape, this applies to every one of you, and do keep it in mind.

What the models wear you can wear if you are tall and slender. Never let a salesperson or a dressmaker persuade you to "cut" your height. Why do you want to look shorter? With sixty-nine inches or more, thank nature's generosity and become a tall, poised beauty.

If you like, you can have enormous sleeves, big collars, intriguing capes, colorful scarves, fur collars, and bell-shaped skirts. Try one of the reversible skirts which turns itself inside out to please you. Other skirts are mentioned in the chapter "Unite and Divide."

The tall, slender girl avoids long tight sleeves and snug-fitting dresses. Evening dresses with swirling bouffant skirts or endless ruffles are attractive.

You can wear fabrics of organdy, taffeta, tweed, corduroy, waffle piqué, velveteen, and all quilted fabrics. Try plaids, horizontal stripes, and tucks. Generally luxuriate yourself in yards of materials and beware of skimpiness or anything itsy-bitsy.

With well-proportioned figures the tall slender and the small slender wear the same lines. It is a matter of proportions. Princess Margaret and the Duchess of Windsor are short but nevertheless famous for their well-dressed appearance. They wear full skirts, coats with a graceful flare, and short evening dresses, all of which are built to their proportions.

The short, slender girl
wears a full skirt
but not a circular one,
which would be too much skirt.

On the other hand, a tall, slender girl
wears the circular skirt.
A cartwheel hat is stunning on the tall girl.
The short girl has one in a smaller edition.
It is simply a matter of dressing to scale.

I don't know why so many of you short, slender girls want to be tall. Your size establishes you as a petite charmer who makes the boys feel big and strong with a yen to look after you; however, there are circumstances where some added height is advantageous and being on the concert stage is one of them.

Lily Pons is one of the most exquisitely dressed women on three continents. Although only five feet tall, she makes use of every one of those inches and by her adroitness adds a few more. Nothing cuts her height, no belts, no sashes, no ruffles, just the long smooth line of a perfectly fitted princess dress. Flowers in her hair or a tiny bewitching hat keeps your eye going up.

When you are short and roly-poly you do need to appear taller and slimmer. Again optical illusion comes to your aid. Vertical lines, sometimes diagonal, are best. Narrow vertical stripes or tucking accent the vertical line. No puff sleeves, no flaring cuffs, no capes and no short, full jackets. For you plump girls large patch pockets are taboo; keep them narrow or have none. Never wear ruffles, plaids, polka dots, or prints; and checks must be small ones. Skirts are "easy," neither pencil slim nor circular. Coats are full length with a modified flare. A straight coat makes you overweight girls appear larger.

Your fabrics are linen, handkerchief linen, batiste,

broadcloth, gabardine, shantung, and chambray. The
materials to avoid are those which increase your size:
corduroy, organdy, tweed, and all fabrics with a nap.
Keep all trimming on your clothes to a minimum, the
less the better.

If you are built on Viking lines (a large well-proportioned figure), you may have difficulty in buying
clothes to fit—designing and making your own is one
solution. Wear cool colors, no polka dots, no checks, no
horizontal tucks, and no circular skirts. Choose simple
clothes with up-and-down lines. When you are beautifully groomed, well-dressed, and with a perfect posture
which you must have, you are beautiful.

I have told you of the slender, tall and short; the
Viking type; and the overweight, tall and short. Let's
now take specific problems which bother many girls.
Let's start with the chin, neck, and collar line.

On paper, draw the shape of your face life size, add a
few strokes of the crayon for the hair; cut dozens of
collars and pin them on the drawing until a pattern is
found which is the best for the shape of your face and
the length of your neck. The Peter Pan collars are
classic and may be shaped many ways, each flattering
to someone. If your face is oval and your neck of average length, any shape is attractive. Here are some hints
for differently shaped chins. When a face is heart-
shaped, beware of points on collars; round the corners.

Neither will the firm-jawed girls wish to duplicate the horizontal chin line. When a line is repeated, it is emphasized.

The problem of the short neck is frequently seen; observe the large number of movie stars who have one. A short neck will look superlatively long if you keep the line from your ear to the shoulder one lovely sweep. Never cut your throat by wearing scarves, choker beads, and high collars. When wearing a little collar be sure it is as low at the base of the neck as possible and that it lies flat. Scooped necklines are most complimentary when they are cut to flatter your chin line—off-the-shoulder dresses are glamorous for you.

A long slender neck wears: chunky costume jewelry, tiny scarves, turtle necks on blouses and sweaters, choker beads. For evening, wear a black velvet band around that slender column, with a flower pendant. You will look as romantic as moonbeams and honeysuckle.

Those of you who are short-waisted need exercises of stretching and bending to keep your waistline supple. Your blouses are simple with vertical stripes or tucks, so the eye is carried up. There should be no fussiness around the neck, no yokes, and no patch pockets. A V-neck or a small, flat collar is becoming. Wide belts are never worn by the short-waisted girls.

The same suggestions hold true if you need a longer-legged look. Pleats and kick pleats in your skirt help to give a vertical feeling, as do rows of buttons. A bolero jacket, being short, doesn't interrupt the long line of the skirt; therefore the skirt seems longer.

Your arms are a trifle long? You are still growing, and in a year or so your arms will be in proportion to the rest of you; however, *now* is important. Long arms attract those spectacularly full sleeves for dress-up. In your casual clothes wear sleeves either half-way between the elbow and shoulder or the three-quarters length. Large cuffs or chunky bracelets are becoming.

When arms seem a trifle short, wear no sleeves or wear long ones. Always, bracelets and cuffs are avoided.

Whether you are tall or short, many of you have slender shoulders and small curves. There are a myriad subtle ways to cope with this problem. Halter necks on sun dresses give more than a hint of fullness. Cape collars, collars with large lapels, fashionable boleros, soft smocking, multiple strands of beads all detract from your flat slenderness. Yokes and dickeys are Houdini touches, by giving the front of your blouses more interest. Jackets or blouses with jeweled buttons, angora or braid-trimmed sweaters give a lovely lift to— your heart. Because you are still growing this slim slim stage is transitory.

Be smart and create the illusion of a well-proportioned figure by using intelligence and imagination.

PRECIOUS LITTLE

Accessories are the little things, the sparkles, which change a drab and dull costume to an attractive one of fashion-plus. More important, accessories should emphasize your outstanding feature. In every work of art there is a focal point, which may be the prettiest, the most interesting, or the most colorful; and always, it catches the attention first.

Your outstanding attraction may be your hair, skin,

eyes, throat, posture, hands, wrists, the perfection of
your face, or the interesting irregularity of your facial
features. At times your best feature may change; for
instance, one suit enhances the color and highlights of
your hair; a dress of another color emphasizes the
beautiful color of your eyes. On the other hand, some
of you have a feature which is so remarkably lovely that
it always attracts attention.

Every feature can no more have the same importance
than Raphael could paint every face in his pictures with
equal emphasis. If he had, the observer's attention
would scatter indiscriminately over every part of the
picture. There must be a focal point, a center of attention, a dominant note (call it whichever you like),
where the beauty and interest is climaxed. Raphael
painted his masterpieces so that the memorably lovely
faces of the Madonna and Child are dominant in his
pictures.

When at the movies, study how the center of interest
(usually, it is the principal actor in a scene) is emphasized with color and contrast. Often the center of interest is a warm color, but when the dominant note is a
cool color, there are warm subdued colors balanced on
each side of it. When the center of interest is light in
value, the background is darker in tone. There is always
a contrast of dark and light to focus your attention. You
soon realize that directors and cameramen are artists.

You, too, will emphasize some feature into an interesting or lovely center of interest. This accomplishment is achieved with forethought and imagination, because accessories come in all sizes and colors from sandals to hair ribbons.

Of the many accessories for your hair, some are attention-getting and others keep your hair inconspicuous. If hair is a nondescript color, keep it a silky, neutral background by matching or harmonizing the accessory with your hair. Color contrast and/or sparkle call attention to lovely hair, and that is what most of you prefer to do by using bright ribbons, flowers, barrettes, or other ornaments.

To keep hair from blowing on your way to dancing, swathe it, pin it, tie it, give it a neat-as-a-pin look in a decorative sort of way, with a large flat ribbon bow across the back of your hair, or across the top, with the tiniest veil. If you live in a frigid zone line a parka hood in a flattering come-hither color or wear an angora hood in a delectable sherbet color, and those blustery winds are no longer a threat. With milder breezes, try a coarse net, sparkled or dull, tied with a ribbon or pinned with a flower.

Flowers draw attention and are to be worn with discrimination. A flower placed near your throat makes a pretty picture. Wearing flowers near the chin line takes thought. Flowers should never be put directly below a

NO

pointed or squarish chin or this is the design. Place them slightly to one side. Flowers, fresh or artificial, or tiny bunches of artificial fruit wired to a velvet ribbon are tried on your hair, at your throat, at the waist, on your purse or wrist. Which feature is to be emphasized? And which feature do you wish to subordinate? Braces on your teeth is the answer from some of you. Because braces are of metal, beware of any accessory which glitters or reflects the light. For that reason pearls are better than a metal necklace.

yes

Some accessories are more expressive than others; the way a shawl, stole, or scarf is worn brings into dominance certain features: posture, hair, skin, eyes, throat, shoulders, or hands. There have been scarves in some form or other for many many years—ever since a cave woman threw a lion skin over one shoulder.

Scarves and shawls have had various names, been made of hundreds of different materials, and worn in many sizes and shapes. In frigid cold or tropical sunshine, luxurious fur or sheer chiffon, they have given an elusive air of mystery and enchantment. No wonder the señoritas have clung to their exquisite lace mantillas these many years. They know the value of lace across pretty shoulders and the contrast with silky black hair.

You, too, with off-the-shoulder or low-necked evening dresses require something ethereal and glamorous around your shoulders to create a beguiling picture.

A fluffy angora stole or cape makes a perfect evening wrap. The color, the length, and the amount of flare are important. Experiment by sketching yourself with different capes and discover which style is best for you.

Sue wears a large hand-woven scarf which has gold metallic threads flashing through it, quite a Midas touch. With a white jersey dress and golden hair she is dynamic and smooth in two colors, gold and white. Mary Lou bought one and a half yards of bright coral terry cloth and finished it with tassels at the ends. With her white bathing suit, golden tanned skin, black hair, and coral stole she is pretty as a picture.

Height is necessary if you wish to wear a large scarf. You can look like something wrapped and not delivered, so choose with finesse and wear with assurance.

Small scarves are versatile, there is no end to their uses and colors. Being near your face, they must flatter your complexion and compliment your eyes. Scarves in muted or singing colors, either in stripes or polka dots, add zest to a winter suit or coat. Either blend or contrast the colors, for scarves are the unexpected accents, the notes which make much of little. A scarf of pale organdy with a spring suit is as cheery as the first robin's chirp. The small silk triangles around your neck add a gay-hearted note to your sweaters, flattering to everyone except those with heavy chins and short necks.

For many of you a wool scarf is a necessity for winter. With a coat of a solid color a striped or plaid scarf adds a stimulating note. A plaid coat, on the other hand, demands a scarf of one color. The same rule is true for plaid, polka dot, and print dresses—this is the time to control any yen for fancy hats, jewelry, shoes, and handbags.

Plastic purses are solid fashion with the school crowd; the cost is small and the care is negligible. Purses with a strap or handles are preferred—the envelopes slip away so easily. A shoulder bag? Change your carrying shoulder or you will become lopsided and then where will your fashion future be? By designing and making your own purse you have one which is truly yours. There are the pouch bags piped with leather, the popular crocheted string bags, the colorful felt purses with a zipper on the inside and a monogram on the outside. A small cosmetic envelope from the nickel-and-dime store is a potential evening bag. Pin on flowers or an enormous glitter pin; paste on your initials or dot it with sequins; for very little, you have something smart and different. At the junior prom the prettiest bag was a small crocheted one completely covered with tiny red and pink silk roses.

Always stress your best features. When a tiny waist belongs to you, wear eye-catching belts and cummerbunds. Let them be the highlights of your accessory collection. Only you can wear the jeweled belts and those with flamboyant buckles. Make a tiny waist piquant with a leopard belt on a gray flannel skirt; a gleaming polished leather belt is perfection on a tweed skirt. A turquoise cummerbund on a blue-violet "date" dress gives an inimitable flair. A slick trick is the reversible belt, two for the price of one and a belt collection in itself. The crazy-quilt belt made of small, brightly colored pieces of flannel is smart with shorts and cotton dresses. A canvas polo belt with a denim skirt gives a casual air. Several lengths of narrow grosgrain ribbon wrapped around your wisp of a waist many times and tied in perky bows is indisputably becoming. When your family and friends discover your penchant for belts, they will be bringing you those with local color, the hand-woven ones from Mexico, the silver girdles from Algiers.

From these places come interesting jewelry. Select your pieces with imagination; they can be gay, imaginative, and serve as conversation pieces. Do keep the cost small because the bulk of your allowance is spent not on the icing but on the bread and butter of your wardrobe—your suits, coats, skirts, and sweaters.

The temptation with all jewelry is to overbuy and to wear indiscriminately. A famous New York jewelry store displays one magnificent piece in the window. Contrast it with the other extreme, the five-and-dime windows. The climax of your suit can be one gorgeous pin in the lapel or a stunning metal choker, never both. Keep it simple.

Avoid jangling bracelets. Other jewelry which is never for school includes earrings, rhinestones, and other glitter.

Gloves give a certain suave finish to an ensemble. Smart and wearable are the string gloves in summer and pigskin gloves in winter. Angora gloves and mittens look heavenly but they shed heartbreakingly.

If your arms are short, gloves should harmonize in color with your long sleeves; when you are bare-armed, the white or pale tan gloves are best.

Another important accessory that is demure, or devastating, is the little white collar, which often leads a double life with more than one outfit. These collars give the touch which lifts a sweater or suit into the "new as April" class. The girls with ample curves cannot wear white collars with lapels.

Some touch of white on many an outfit is what gives it non-stop appeal: sweet, chic, or flauntingly crisp. A white embroidered organdy scarf, white gloves, and white costume jewelry give a dark or neutral-colored suit that exquisitely fresh look.

It's smart to integrate your wardrobe around one color; remember the law of "one color predominates"? If your coat or suit is navy blue, that is the dominant color; your accessories are highlighted or blended with it. Here is an integrated color ensemble. A navy suit is the background; the blouse, shoes, and bag are navy blue. The white hat is trimmed with blue and red. The gloves are white and the scarf is red and white. Attention is centered on the face, which is between the red hat decoration and the red in the scarf; the two reds balance.

This is Marian's color harmony with her navy suit. She chooses pink and red, which are sharp and sweet together. The blouse, gloves, and one flower are pink. The shoes, hat, and another flower are red. Being tall, Marian wears hat and shoes of the same color, which contrasts with the dominant color, navy blue.

Always have an accessory to match the dominant color. How many colors with your "main" color? The general rule is two or three. A mimosa yellow is stunning with chocolate brown or navy. Combined with black patent leather and gray, mimosa is something to cheer about. Try cerise with biscuit color or turquoise with sand. Experiment until you are thrilled with the color harmony.

Accessories proclaim your individual style. This is particularly true when different girls wear the identical dress. Each girl, by choosing her own accessories, makes the dress undeniably hers. The same accessory, on the other hand, can be worn by two girls and the effect is very different on each. Try on your complete outfit before a long mirror; make everything you wear a definite contribution to your smoothness and discard the rest. Simplicity is smartness.

Another accessory is an intriguing whiff of perfume. It's the certain sparkle which sends your spirits winging. Light and delicate flower aromas are sparkling, demure, or flirtatious. The heavy, spicy, musky, and exotic scents are ridiculous with your fresh, smooth, look, which requires a light flower fragrance.

You occasionally prefer to be identified with one certain scent, but with so many alluring fragrances there is no need to be an echo of yourself. Once upon a time, all the girls in a club decided to use the same perfume. A sad mistake!

An adroit touch of perfume gives a provocative fragrance for hours when it is touched to the inside of your elbows, to your wrists, the base of your throat, and back of the ears. Exquisite fragrances are delightful.

So off you go with a host of heavenly ideas!

UNITE AND DIVIDE

Separate and divide equals multiplication. Double-talk? Yes! It's fantastic; it's magic. It's fun in every division: dresses, suits, jackets, skirts, sweaters, beach togs, evening dresses, and pajamas, too. Separates take the highest rating. Why? Because they make an integrated and functional wardrobe individually yours. Their number is increased at little cost; in fact, you can "prime the pump" yourself with some material and a little energy. Parenthetically, the sooner a sewing machine is a part of your life, the more clothes you may have. Smart girls invest their money in the classics: a really good tweed suit, an excellently tailored flannel skirt, and sweaters. The budget for party dresses is kept low, a glamorous effect being necessary but durability unimportant.

The number of roles "separates" play depends upon your imaginative ability to switch and swap. Friends are intrigued with your enthusiasm for contrasting, harmonizing, or matching fabrics and colors with your clothes.

The height, weight, and proportions of a figure are easily changed with a wardrobe of separates. Jackets and skirts of the same cool color slenderize the plump girl. The tall brunette with the yellow blouse and red skirt appears shorter than when she wears a light blue sweater and blue skirt. The sweater can be worn with

the red skirt; the yellow blouse can be "united" with the blue skirt. Remember in "color magic" what you learned about choosing colors?

Slim girls with twenty-inch waists are fortunate, because a voluminous skirt with a cummerbund and blouse equals enchantment. Another time, for a party, wear a nylon net overskirt, sprinkled with tiny velvet flowers or border it with silk field flowers. Daisies or tiny velvet bows in various colors could polka dot it.

Wear a different top with your skirt and you look as different and as new as now. Have a satin blouse with a scooped neckline, a little sweater (a ribbon collar can be added), or a white organdy blouse with enormous, full sleeves and a little round collar. Remember that these tops can be worn with bouffant skirts, too.

A pretty skirt for summer is candy-striped cotton

with a blouse in one of the candy colors. A short circular skirt is graceful, and if you are really tiny-waisted, try a short piqué skirt with unpressed pleats. One of the prettiest is an aqua skirt with a white blouse bound around the neck with the aqua piqué.

Beach togs may seem a far cry from dresses, but this is a mistaken idea in the story of separates. It's being done by the more imaginative designers. Four "sea separates" come from two tops and two shorts. A pretty mix-up is a bra of flowered cotton broadcloth with striped cotton shorts. Since beach clothes lead double lives, it's important to harmonize them with the rest of your wardrobe. The same white piqué halter which goes to the beach goes with a summer skirt to lunch and dancing later. A good-looking halter is indefinitely versatile. Beach coats are cut on very smart lines and can be used over summer dresses. Is white one of your important colors? By all means have a white bolero which completes many combinations, with a skirt, a halter, or sleeveless blouse in any color, or keep it an all-white ensemble. The chapter "Summer Icicles" gives other ideas about beach clothes.

Swimming isn't the only sport where separates are vital. Classics on the golf course are: the gored skirt, the pull-over, belted sweater, the trim shirt, the middy, and the tailored two-piece cottons. They contribute serviceability with true fashion.

White is the accepted color for tennis players. If you wear a skirt, don't get it too short; one which just clears the knee is more graceful. Shorts must be large enough to give you freedom to dash for the ball. Colored lingerie is strictly out.

Be trim and look like an expert. Buy your clothes carefully. The shirts and dresses must have easy armholes, with extra width across the shoulders which will let you stretch and swing. Separates allow more freedom around the waist, too. They are relaxingly comfortable.

Sports are fun but school is part of your life, too. The foundation of school clothes is sweaters and skirts, blouses and skirts. Often what seems a soft little jersey dress is a blouse and skirt. Synthetic fibers are playing an important role in all fabrics because of their serviceability, and the fact that they are easy to launder.

Three on a match are: a beige jersey skirt, permanently pleated, with a jacket of the same material, plus a navy wool shirt or a yellow middy. It's like dominoes—one separate leads to another.

Choose your clothes carefully and they will serve you well—in every situation.

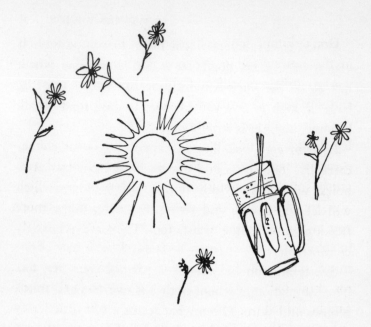

SUMMER ICICLES

When the sun is at its zenith, and the days are at their warmest, sunlight fashions and perfect grooming transform you into a summer charmer. This immaculately crisp and cool appearance is worth capturing, so make it yours.

Never, never gasp and sigh about the heat. When the others do—and they will—you talk about something else. Any yen for arguments is controlled. Why cause your circulation to hurry?

Don't slump, don't collapse like a broken accordion in the nearest swing. No one is interested in seeing you go to pieces except Dennis the Menace. Swing, and sip your iced drinks, but there's sugar in those; the more calories, the more heat your body generates. Icy drinks also interfere with the body's normal temperature-regulating action. Cold drinks poured *incessantly* into your stomach are dangerous.

A steaming cup of tomato bouillon doesn't make you as hot as a ham sandwich does, which is higher in calories. However, and this is important, your swimming, tennis, and picnics take energy, so every day eat three balanced meals to which more fruit juices can be added.

Eat and chatter, but don't lie around in that swing all day while the others groan, "It's too hot to lift an eyelash." Get up and move around and you are cooler.

Doing things in hot weather makes staying dainty a problem. Bathe and shower more often; a lukewarm shower leaves you cooler than a cold one, which increases the circulation. Pat, don't rub dry, sprinkle talcum here and there, or spray refreshing cologne over yourself with a lavish hand. These luxuries give that fresh-as-a-daisy feeling which you intend to keep —at least for a while.

Anti-perspirants and deodorants are your aids. The liquid kind seems to be the surest safeguard. Make it a habit to use an anti-perspirant or deodorant every night, because if it is used in the daytime any moving about may start you perspiring, and the effectiveness is washed away. Some girls prefer a cream deodorant: remember that finger tips must be scrupulously clean before you dip into the jar, because underarms are susceptible to infection; never wipe under the arms with a used tissue or handkerchief. If you have to shave under your arms, follow the directions on the package or wait for a while before using either a deodorant or an anti-perspirant.

Apply your lipstick lightly with a brush to give the edges a neat line; the chapter "Let's Face It" tells how. The lipstick color is correct if it harmonizes with your tanned skin. A delicate porcelain pink lipstick is the beguiling answer if you don't tan.

Hair is brushed back and up. Braid it, pin it, tie it, or cut it short. Quaint, natural, or sophisticated, make it smooth and neat.

Summer clothes are made from many different fabrics, all of them wash like a breeze and some need no ironing. The coolest and airiest fabrics are voile, sheer handkerchief linen, breezy batiste, and eyelet cottons. Seersuckers and denim are smart for casual clothes; let them be crisp, not clingy.

Some colors give a feeling of coolness, as an icy blue and a pale green. Poppy and nasturtium colors are flattering to many girls, but when the weather is muggy, as well as hot, use those colors seldom. There are three "schools of thought" concerning colors for summer clothes. Most of you belong to two of them.

The first is the "all white" or "white with colored accessories school." Crisp white goes beautifully with a tanned skin, and for practicality it is tops—there is no danger of white material fading in the sun or in the laundry. A crisp white outfit is as spectacular as an icicle at a Fourth of July picnic.

Pastel colors, which are mentioned in the chapter "Color Magic," constitute the second "school of thought." The frosted monotones, the fragrant spring colors of apple blossom pink, cool frosty green, lilac, lime green, cool blue, and the palest of lemon yellow are exquisite when they flatter you.

The third "school of color magic" is composed of the "sun-drenched" colors, sometimes called the Mediterranean hues. They can hold their own in the most brilliant sun, against the bluest water and the whitest sand. These gorgeous hues all demand a vivid personality in the wearer; otherwise these strong colors will overshadow you. Try these colors on yourself.

No matter which colors you wear you have your place in the sun. The sun warms and relaxes your body and mind. When sun-bathing, be careful and don't fry. A hazy overcast day is misleading, the rays are there, reaching through to burn you. A sky polka-dotted with fleecy white clouds is more dangerous than a bright blue sky. The best time of day to "sun" is early and late, avoiding the sun between eleven o'clock and three.

Fair-skinned girls burn worse and need extra precautions. Five or ten minutes of sun the first day are enough; the exposure time is gradually increased. Other girls take it slowly too, although they can start with fifteen minutes a day and increase the time slightly faster.

If you have been taking sulfa drugs be careful about sun-bathing, and if there are any reactions, do see your doctor.

A bad burn can result in infection, or chills and fever; then it's a hospital for you. Treat the lesser burns with an unguent from the drugstore or cover the burned area with a thin paste of soda and water. Stay out of the sunshine until the burn is completely healed; a burn on a burn is painful. The advertisements tell about sun-tan lotions and creams. Some encourage a golden-bronze hue; other lotions block out the sun's ultraviolet rays and are for the girls with sensitive skins. Many girls mix their own formula of half olive oil and half vinegar. No dried skins, no peeled noses, or swollen lips with the extra precaution of sun lotions or baby oil.

Your hair can be braided in pigtails and pinned securely to your head, no hair in your eyes while you are swimming. What summer sun and swimming can do to nice hair! After swimming always wash the salt or chlorine out of your hair before it dries.

Are you a bathing-cap devotee? Stack your hair on top, keeping it farthest from the water, and tie a dampened strip of chamois around your head at the hairline. With a bathing cap on no water can get to the top of your head.

Suits are brief and comfortable, taking sun, water, and sand. Other beach togs are described in the chapter "Unite and Divide."

Here's fun to you on hot sunny days!

LET'S FACE IT

Did you ever spend an hour in the art museum with the statues of ancient Greece? All those perfect oval faces! Monotonous, aren't they? I am positive that Artemis really had a piquant heart-shaped face. And if just once Athena had one eyebrow higher than the other, how much more interesting her expression!

The more fascinating faces are those which are round, heart- or diamond-shaped, and those with a firm jaw. Analyze your face and discover which type is yours. No matter what the shape, every face can be attractively framed by following some of these suggestions, which you adapt to suit yourself. To make a general rule uniquely yours is the secret of individuality.

Tall, slim girls should have a hair-do which doesn't add height. Tiny girls need a hair style which is scaled to their size; being small, they know that it is easy to be top-heavy with waves and curls. Overweight girls strike a happy medium with trim, well-cut hair. When hair is pulled back tightly or the waves and curls are voluminous, the head isn't in balance with a heavy figure.

Bangs are adaptable to many shapes of faces. When cut straight across, bangs camouflage a high or low forehead. Bangs may be straight, curly, or fluffy, and go all or part of the way across the forehead. Whether a face is shortened or lengthened depends upon the style of the bangs.

If a firm jaw gives you a horizontal line, have slightly curled bangs which go part way across the forehead.

Do sharp, pointed features and a thin face belong to you? Let soft waves of hair come to the shoulders, no sleekness but silky waving softness. Gail has her amber-colored hair in a long bob which fills out her narrow jaw line and chin. If Gail's hair were black, the long bob would be impossible for her to wear because the strong contrast of black hair and light skin would emphasize her pointed chin.

Chubby faces are round when framed with a short fluffy bob. The hair should be brushed up and back from the temples, with a wave added at the side of the forehead. And the face is no longer round.

If your features are rather large, let your hair have loose waves which balance and soften the severity of your features.

By having a wave or lock of hair on one side of the forehead, you diminish the width across the top of your face.

Now some suggestions about the profile. If you have a large nose, you should never wear a pony tail on the same line as the nose or the nose seems very large. With a receding chin and forehead, let a bang puff out over the forehead, show the ears, and the chin will count for more.

The part of the hair plays an important role in lengthening or broadening the face. A center part lengthens the face, the forehead, and the nose, because the vertical line of the part carries the eye up. The direction of line in a hair-do is just as important as it is in designing clothes. None of the movie stars, men or women, has a part which goes straight back from the starting point on the forehead. For round- and square-shaped faces the part starts at the crown and comes forward diagonally. A long, slender face needs the opposite angle. These slanting parts are also excellent for those faces with irregular features.

Draw your face, life-size, and with a few crayon strokes sketch in the hair. Or with a comb and brush try your hair different ways and look in the mirror. Experiment with many hair styles until you find "your own."

The simpler a hair style, the more attractive it is; in every case keep it smooth and never never fussy. Most of you conservatively keep the same hair style too long. A different hair-do may reveal new beauty in your hair and face. Whether your hair covers your head in short curls, a pert pixie cut, smooth braids, or a long bob, do yourself a good turn by finding the styles which are most becoming to you.

After your face is framed to perfection, the next goal is a beautiful complexion. Most of you teen-agers have normal skins and you are smart to keep them that way with good health. Cleanliness is the foundation of grooming. Clean, cleaner, cleanest you learn in grammar, but when it comes to you, it isn't true. You are either clean or you aren't.

Fill your hands with warm suds and gently wash every inch of your face and neck. Lather those suds in the creases of your chin and in those around your nose, or someday tiny hard granules will appear in those congested pores. Rinse and rinse in warm water, finishing off with cool. After tennis and basketball wash your face thoroughly; never let perspiration dry on it.

If you have acne, don't scratch. Ask a doctor's advice. One famous dermatologist (doctor for the skin) does not accept a patient with a "bad" complexion unless she promises to walk five miles a day in the fresh air. It's good health which gives a beautiful glow to your skin and a sparkle to your eyes.

Eyes, too, have "frames," the eyebrows. Bring your brows under control with a tiny brush and a touch of vaseline. Brush them in the opposite direction from which they grow, brush them up and finally smooth them down. Carefully pluck the stray hairs from under the brows and those which tend to meet across the bridge of the nose. Some girls hold a damp, warm washcloth or a piece of cotton dipped in witch hazel over the area before they start to pluck; other girls rub an ice cube lightly over the skin. In either case be sure your hands and tweezers are antiseptically clean, and after tweezing carefully use a touch of witch hazel on the plucked places.

More complexion flattery? Your lipstick is one of the beguiling answers. Choose and buy inexpensive small lipsticks so you can have several to match and harmonize with the different colors you wear.

Apply the lipstick carefully to your lips; clean-cut, symmetrical curves are prettiest. No frayed, feathered, or smudged edges, so it's a lipstick brush for you. A brush takes too long? Ten or fifteen minutes' practice and the technique is yours. Starting with a clean brush, stroke the brush back and forth on the stick to get plenty of color. Rest your elbow on the table, holding the brush as a pencil, little finger resting against your chin, starting at the center of the bow, and with one sweep go to the corner; repeat on the other side. Do the lower lip in one stroke. Practice for a quick precision and the result is a clean-cut outline which will keep its shape all day. Brush the color in lightly until smooth and it will be neither caked nor shiny. The

shape of your mouth can be changed *slightly,* but usually *the natural line of your lips is followed.*

Keeping the mouth in the background is, alas, too true of the girl with a dish-shaped face. Her mouth is "set back," so an inconspicuous lipstick is needed. It should be a light true red or slightly toward an orange shade because these are forward colors.

Sometimes one side of the mouth is slightly irregular; build it out and modify it to match the other, staying as close to the natural line as possible. These suggestions are to be used with common sense.

Finally there is the girl with a droopy mouth. Why not smile? Just naturally droopy! Don't believe it.

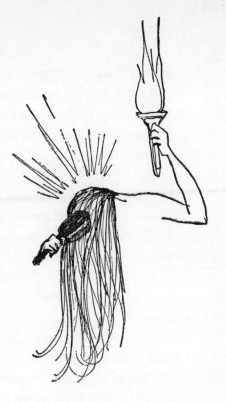

YOUR HEADLIGHT
IS YOUR HAIR

Healthy, clean, and shining hair catches admiring glances because the prettiest thing on your head is your hair.

In a poll taken of 969 high-school students, 22 per cent of the girls and 20 per cent of the boys voted that the most annoying grooming trait of a girl was unkempt hair. With this evidence it behooves every girl to study her hair with a critical and appraising eye.

Hair tells all, too. Haven't you noticed your hair after a bout with the flu? Oh, the dullness and the limpness of it! All the permanents in the world won't hide sickly hair, those brittle ends, the fuzzy curls, the stringiness, the dandruff, and the dullness. These can't be camouflaged.

But take heart, for there is nothing which responds so quickly to loving care as your hair. Along with the right food, plenty of sleep, and sunny fresh air you brush, brush, and brush. Use a brush with long medium-firm bristles and keep it immaculate—wash it every night, if necessary.

Bend over from the waist, so the blood goes to the scalp and nourishes the hair, place the brush firmly against your scalp, and in a long sweeping motion brush to the tips of your hair. Here is a warning note. If your scalp isn't accustomed to this vigorous brushing, take it slowly, say fifteen or twenty strokes at a time, and gradually in a few weeks increase it to four or five hundred strokes during the course of a day or evening. Twice-a-day brushing is better than once-a-day and the best of all is brushing scattered through your waking hours. Play a favorite record and brush and brush. Telephoning? Brush. Relaxing in a tub of warm water? Brush those locks.

Sometimes girls are shocked to see how much hair is left in the brush. Relax and remember you do lose some hair every day; that's an accumulation of dead hair which you are carrying around! Ugh!

When Katharine Hepburn arrived in Hollywood the first time, she was startled to be told that her hair didn't photograph well. Carrying a brush everywhere, she used it. Now look at her hair, a silken cloud. Use your brush and compliments will soon start coming your way.

While hair is brushed, the scalp is also being stimulated and the oil glands are kept normal, all of which destroys that dry-hair bugaboo some of you have. And no wonder, with dry furnace heat in winter and the strong rays of the summer sun, hair can resemble straw.

Dry hair and skin are helped by eating an extra pat of butter, drinking milk, and using salad oil on heaping plates of greens. And there are other improvements for dry hair. Olive oil, lanolin, or a commercial hair-conditioning cream helps the dryness and split ends. Divide the hair in sections and rub the warm oil or cream on your scalp; massage gently. A damp, warm towel wrapped around the head relieves a dry, taut scalp.

A few of you have oily hair, the kind that catches and holds every bit of grime and dirt which floats your way. Oh yes, oily hair is brushed. A week or so and the hair is oilier because the brushing carries the oil down to the ends of the hair. But at the same time the oil glands

are being stimulated back to normal. If you have oily hair eat plenty of green leafy vegetables, drink several glasses of water, and give butter a light touch or only a passing glance.

There's more to a lovely head of hair than just wishing, isn't there? Clean it must be. The frequency of shampooing depends upon the amount of dust and grime in the hair, as well as the condition of the scalp. Oily hair demands more frequent washing than dry. If you are living in the country, where the air is clean, a shampoo every ten days is a good average. A city gal? Once a week or more.

Before shampooing collect everything necessary—a small stiff brush to clean the hairline, towels, and a cup of suds. Rubbing a cake of soap on those locks is taboo. There are good shampoos in the stores, including the detergent shampoos which are excellent for hard water, the kind which has a high mineral content; with this type of shampoo the rinsing is easier and quicker. Your own shampoo can be made by dissolving a bar of mild soap in hot water. While watching it melt into bubbly suds, you can be brushing your hair to remove any loosened dandruff and grime.

Washing hair under a shower is the easiest way, but in the absence of a shower a spray can be attached to the faucet; however, there are thousands of girls who wash their hair in the washbasin or a large pan. Elaborate equipment isn't a guarantee of better results.

Soap in the eyes? Have a damp washcloth handy. Suds on your clothes? Add an extra towel or plastic cape to your collection.

Don't miss a fraction of an inch on your scalp, especially those neglected places around the hairline and back of the ears. A vigorous shampoo causes the circulation to gallop and leaves a clean, stimulated scalp.

Rinse and rinse again. Start with warm water and taper off to cool. Rinsing with a spray is the easiest way. If you haven't a spray get an ordinary sprinkling can. Paint it, keep it as a decorative note on the shelf, and you'll be looked upon as a clever girl with a will to find a way.

When using an electric dryer
make sure it is warm
and never hot.
The best method of drying hair
is to brush it dry
in the warm sunshine.
The brushing dry
helps to bring out
the natural wave.
Most healthy hair
does have a natural wave
which can be coaxed into

something very attractive, so while your hair is slightly damp, brush and pull your waves into place. When pin curls are necessary, pat them with a towel to hasten drying, and remove the pins as soon as possible. To spare your public the sight of pin curls, wrap a coarse net of a becoming color around your head. And you should never wear pin curls when you go out!

For a sleek effect rub a few drops of brilliantine or a creamy hair lotion between your palms and then rub your palms over your hair while it is still damp. Straight hair can be "sharp"! If nature gave you really straight hair, she also gave you harmonizing features. Straight hair can look stunning or very chic. Remember what you learned about styling your hair.

When there isn't time for a shampoo and a smooth look is necessary on a moment's notice, here is a hint to keep your grooming perfect. The hair is parted every inch and swabbed with a hair-cleansing preparation; wrap a piece of cheesecloth around your brush and use it in the accustomed way. Next turn the ends of your hair on curlers and lightly spray them with a quick setting-lotion—some girls prefer cologne if their hair is oily. By the time you are dressed, your hair is as neat as always.

Beautiful hair is yours—if you want it.

DANGEROUS CURVES

Curves—Coming and Going

You can have dimples and your eyelashes may curl from here to yon, but if you are a fatty, you aren't a beau-catcher. It's a family trait to be overweight? Don't be ridiculous. You aren't the petite type, but those extra pounds are no help. It's time to use will power and here's the way to start.

Stand in front of a full-length mirror without your clothes. What do you think of that fat tummy, those padded legs, and balloon arms? Under that layer of fat is a beautiful slender body which is *yours*. Never will you see it unless you want it. You say, "Of course, I do." Honestly, do you? Think it over, the decision is yours.

Dieting is no picnic; neither is it so difficult. Talk it over with your mother and think it through with your doctor. Never start unless you intend to finish. Either do it or stop talking and wishing that you were slim and graceful.

A wish-wash? All right, sit in a corner and watch the gang with their good times. You'll develop a sullen mouth, unhappy eyes, sloppy posture, and a waddling walk. Who cares? Oh no, not you, wish-wash.

You have decided to do it. All reducing must be done under a doctor's care. Off you go to the doctor for a diet tailored to your weight, height, bone structure, and glandular system. The doctor also prescribes exercises or approves the ones you need. Although you are active and will become more so as the fat vanishes, you must exercise to prevent flabbiness. Exercise is a circulation rouser, forcing out the fatigue and food poisons as well as burning fatty tissues. The result is good muscle tone and a beautiful shape.

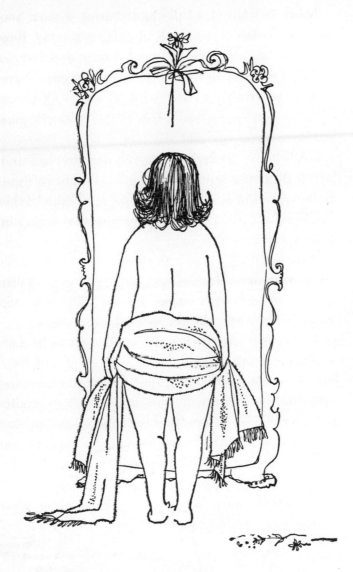

Swimming is one of the best all-around exercises; and here arises a problem, the increasing of your appetite. After any exercise milk or buttermilk demolishes the craving for food, particularly sweets. For some of you fruit juice curbs the appetite.

At home there are two kinds of exercises, the ones you do as exercises and the others, called "keeping house." Both slenderize. The carpet sweeper and broom slim your arms; scrubbing shelves firms those flabby arms. But is there a growling about hips? Hips are always the first cry, but a poor posture resulting in a "stick out" tummy is more prevalent and is far worse for your health.

Because hips receive the most consideration from you teen-agers, here's an exercise. Lie on your back and lift your legs and mid-section in the air, the weight resting on your shoulders, hands under your waist, and elbows on the floor. Start bicycling. Repeat until you feel pleasantly stretched. A warning—never exercise until you are exhausted. Start slowly and gradually increase the time.

This is easy to do. Standing, rest right hand on back of chair, swing left leg forward and back. Keep leg straight. Start with four times, then rest left hand on chair and repeat with the right leg. Work up to twenty-five times.

Down on the floor you go. Lie on your back with knees bent and together. Arms outstretched at sides, pull in abdominal muscles. Keep shoulders flat on floor, turn knees and slap legs on floor, first on the right side and alternate to the left.

Here is the "scooter" and one of the best and easiest for hips. Sit on the floor, arms outstretched in front, and "walk" across the room on your buttocks ("sitting bones").

More? Stand erect in a comfortable stance, arms outstretched at sides, swing body to the left, and, without bending your knees, touch your right fingers to your left toes. Stand erect and touch your right toes with your left hand. Stretch free and easy.

You can "slice the middle" by standing on tiptoe, stretching up and up. Feel it slim your waist?

These exercises will give you more vitality and a slimmer figure. The improvements start at once; the first week the waistbands of your skirts have to be adjusted. Aren't you happy as they become smaller and smaller? A practical solution to clothes alteration is a dress which hangs straight from the shoulders. A belt is added to give it shape.

Only five or six pounds overweight? Start exercising and stop those in-between snacks and gooey desserts. In place of sodas and candy have milk or tomato juice.

When Ann decided to lose her surplus fourteen pounds, she went to the drugstore for a double banana split. The instant the last spoonful disappeared she was on her doctor's diet, which was to last six weeks. Not once did she break over. At first there was teasing and deliberate tempting, which wasn't cricket, but when the other students realized her determination, they came out with cheers. Now she is slim; she is devastating. You, too, can attain your goal.

If you aren't encased in too much fat, your doctor can predict when the extra pounds will be gone, so set yourself a definite date and work toward it. It could be your birthday party, Thanksgiving dance, Easter parade, or the Fourth of July picnic. No matter the day, here's cheers to you for your accomplishment.

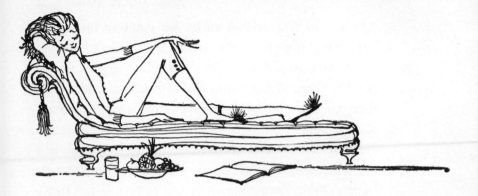

CURVES AHEAD

You ultraslender girls can conceal your lack of weight with ruffles; who wants to be smothered in ruffles all the time? The important question you ask is, "How do I gain weight?"

Many of you slim teens are emotionally tense; now is the time to start your common sense functioning. You want happy, carefree living, but your worry, rushing, and lack of organization all contribute to tension. Remove tension and you digest your food, sleep better, and start to gain. You worry over problems which grow fantastically in your imagination. Talk them over with your parents, your grandmother, or your older brother or sister. Don't whine and don't harp; take a time when you can "talk it out."

Is it a course at school which has you on edge? The boy who is friendly but who just won't ask you for a date? Your family, too, has had these upsets. Once upon a time, Mother and Father were your age and dating. Impossible? It happened. Now they want you to have fun.

After your worries are on the way to being solved, ask your doctor for a checkup; your lack of weight may have a physical cause which he can correct. If you have normal health but are too slender, he will give you a diet and prescribe some exercises for better circulation and muscle tone.

Doctors insist on three balanced meals with a snack now and then. If you have been doing without breakfast, you are living on illusions and "nerves." Your vitality is lowered. No wonder math isn't for you and the third period seems endless. By that time of day the only people you like can be counted on two fingers. When eating breakfast allow enough time to sit and eat without gulping. Drink your fruit juice, eat your cereal, egg, and toast. Enjoy breakfast and you will be ready for the day.

Relax whenever you can. Lie down fifteen minutes before dinner. Make yourself go completely limp and try to float off to sleep. After dinner lie down quietly ten or fifteen minutes to give your digestion an opportunity to function.

Another help for this gain of pounds and energy is the after-school and bedtime snack. A glass of creamy milk or cheese and crackers may be the nourishment you need. Patty, with her bedtime snack of bowl of half cream and half milk with soda crackers, gained five pounds the first month.

Sleeping eight or nine hours gives you that wide-awake feeling in the morning. To sleep relaxingly comfortable, take an all-over stretch; lie flat, push your heels down and your head way up, and stretch.

Another relaxer is this one: stand with feet apart and let the trunk drop forward from the waist. Swing trunk upward, arms overhead, then down again. Swing up and down as relaxed as a sleepy kitten.

Here's a figure maker. Stand with feet together, arms outstretched at sides, shoulder level, palms down; make circles in the air. Your first swing will be backward. Repeat the circles with palms up, swinging in the same direction. The hollows at your shoulders and collarbone will disappear.

Your doctor should check your exercises. Work into any exercises gradually; never let yourself become stiff. If you like, do them to music; dancing is best of all. If there is a class at school or the Y.W.C.A., enroll today. If there isn't, dance at home by yourself, let the music flow through you and improvise your steps. You are becoming graceful—and it's fun.

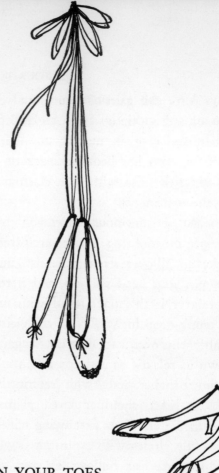

ON YOUR TOES

Comfortable feet give a carefree swing to your walk, a happy lilt to your dancing, and sturdy endurance for a hike. But when your feet are in pain, the results are: a strained face, tortured eyes, and a curdled disposition. Essential to your comfort are a snug, well-fitted arch and the right amount of toe room. When buying shoes always have the salesman measure your feet, because you are still growing. Your size will probably be different from that of six months ago.

Being wise, you buy low-heeled oxfords which have iron constitutions and are eager to lead an active life. For school shoes there are always the classic colors, black and brown, often combined with white. In addition there are other colors which are keyed to the prevailing fashion picture. The warm colors are attractive, but your feet appear larger in red shoes than those shoes in green, blue, black, or brown colors.

For dancing, no doubt, you have made much ado about the tall heels. With such extreme heels you don't make a sophisticated appearance—instead you give an excellent imitation of a teeter-totter tottering. To prevent this, the designers and manufacturers have come up with a smart shoe with a mid-high heel which appears gracefully higher. These pumps, which are feather-light and heavenly comfortable, are chosen because dancing shoes must encourage a graceful walk and let you float away to the music.

For a completely smooth, heel-to-toe picture, consider the background. "My socks are immaculate and my shoes are plus-perfect," you reply. But, those knees! Yes, you did kneel on the gym floor and on the rocks and ashes at the last wiener roast, but why should your knees tell the grimy past? And those tiny scaly bumps! Besides, that pebbled effect certainly will be conspicuous with those wisps of sheer nylons which you received for your birthday.

Into the bathroom you go, and here's the equipment needed: stiff nail brush, bath oil or cold cream, salt, and talcum. No quick swish, swish, either. You are scrubbing your legs and feet completely and thoroughly clean with warm suds and brushes, giving a special scouring to all the trouble spots; the shinbones, the knees, around the toenails, the heels, and everywhere else just make it unanimous. If your legs are rough and scaly, rub them while wet with a handful of salt to smooth them. Rinse, dry your feet carefully, see that no moisture remains between the toes. Massage bath oil or cold cream on your feet, and finish with a fragrant hand lotion. That sandpaper effect can't be changed at once, but with ten days of care those legs will become smooth.

Always your legs are kept non-fuzzy, and for this

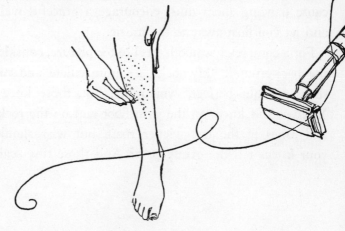

there are many depilatories in the stores with which you can experiment. Pumice paper is used when the hair growth is light, but the quickest and easiest way is shaving cream and a razor.

The rub-a-dub-dub, relaxing massage, and soothing lotion are a comfortable beginning. The finishing touch is a pedicure. If you are giving yourself a manicure at the same time, do the pedicure first lest your fingernail polish be smeared or nicked. Push the cuticle of the toenails back with a cotton-covered orange stick dipped in cuticle remover. Cut the nails straight across and finish with a light brushing of an emery board to avoid the possibility of any snaggle edges. Massage any excess cream around the nails. And remember, this grooming isn't done in the rush hours of the bathroom while the family's tempers soar.

Socks for school and alluring wisps of nylons for dress-up are very much taken for granted. A well-informed clerk can tell which brand is best for you. The lengths of hose are proportioned for different heights; in addition, there are the knee-length hose with elastic at the top, which are a favorite with many of you. The size of your stocking is of the utmost importance; be sure you buy socks and hose at least a half inch longer than your foot. Whether hose are long or short, wide or narrow, they all take careful handling.

A snag is a stocking's worst enemy. Wearing gloves —rayon ones are best—gather the stocking in your two hands to the ankle, put one thumb back of the seam, gently pull the stocking up straight, and fasten it to your garters. A garter belt or girdle is put on absolutely straight.

With dresses of bright-colored calicoes, plaid ging-hams, and candy-striped piqués, the smooth gold or bronze, bare-legged effect is perfect for many times and different places.

But why so downcast? Your legs are not your best feature? Take heart, you can be helped with exercise, diet, and camouflage. Your legs are large? On the scales you go. Hm, only slightly over your quota, but those little fatty pads around your ankles must go. Fight the bulge with a reducing diet—some exercises to tone the muscles—and watch the fat disappear. Sit on the floor with legs stretched out in front: heels resting on the floor. The toes curled tightly under, pull foot back from ankle. Relax. Extend foot forward, toes leading, and grip with toes. Relax and do it with the other foot. Repeat three or four times and gradually increase the number to twenty or twenty-five times.

Swimming is the best sport to slenderize legs and ankles. The strenuous exercises of tennis, hiking, or golf develop the leg muscles which become firmer and larger, and are for those girls with normal and slender legs.

With problem legs skirts are still worn where fashion dictates. Some girls mistakenly wear their skirts long, thinking their legs will not be so noticeable. Long skirts call attention to themselves and raise the question "Why so long?" Then comes the appraising look at your legs. When legs are large, wear hose in the darkest shade which *is in style*. The light, warm copper tones are flattering for the very slender legs. But, more important, stay with the colors in the fashion picture.

Knock-kneed or bowlegged? You are young enough for the doctor to do something about it. Corrective shoes help and are built so no one can guess.

Keep your problems inconspicuous and play up another part of you, and soft-pedal your faults.

The short feet well-padded with muscles kick up their heels and breeze along. It's the long, bony feet which are easily overworked and underprivileged; treasure and pamper them intelligently.

Well-groomed legs, comfortable feet, smart, well-fitting shoes give you a feeling of assurance as you walk lightheartedly on the sunny side of the street.

HERE'S A WISH

If there were *only one* wish I could give to you, it would be an erect, gracefully smooth walk. A perfect carriage tells: flawless co-ordination, lithe muscles, vitality, health, poise, and the ability to wear clothes well. The way you walk and stand mirrors your feelings of happiness, buoyancy, discouragement, or indifference; the ones which belong to you can't be hidden. Truly all emotions can be expressed without words.

The posture and gestures of an actor establish the

emotional pattern which he is projecting across the foot-
lights. I shall never forget a moment in *The Merchant
of Venice,* when not a word was spoken. It was toward
the end of the fourth act, when Shylock is utterly de-
feated by Portia and the Duke. You felt the terrible
futility of Shylock's rage: that cruel and cunning man
met the tremendous climax of his life with failure, and
only tragedy could follow. He looked despairingly at
his bright, clean knife and very, very slowly turned and
left the stage. His hatred followed like a shadow. In
that large theater the breathless, absolute silence reached
out and gripped every one of us in its tragic spell.

Control is the inflexible core of acting. There are
many actresses who move with smooth distinction because their bodies never unconsciously tighten or jerk
with tense muscles. An illustration which comes to
mind is—Jennifer Jones running in the wind, so buoy-
ant and alive she is part of the wind and the hurrying
clouds.

Eager to start? First, line up your spinal column.
No, no, it isn't *that* stiff. In fact, it isn't stiff at all, because the twenty-six uneven vertebrae are held together in long, shallow curves with a few ligaments.
The spinal column supports your rib cage, lungs, and
the abdominal organs. The spinal column stays erect
because the muscles of the legs and those along your
back support it. Keep this girdle of muscles lithe,

strong, and firm with exercise, and you will never have a thick flabby waistline.

Stand in front of a mirror and line yourself up with head and rib cage balanced directly over your hips, and knees slightly flexed. Never lock those knees or out pops your tummy in front and out bounces your fanny in the rear. Center that rib cage, fold your hips down and under; your shoulders and chest are left alone. Your weight is on the arch between the heels and toes. Easy does it!

The best exercise to help you center your head, rib cage, and hips is to stand three or four inches away from a wall or door with knees deeply bent and separated. Press your waistline against the door and push slowly up along the wall until your legs are almost straight. Lift up your chest and pull your chin in so there is the smallest possible space between the door and the back of your neck. You can't keep this line-up all the time and don't try, but every little while line yourself up and start off again.

For better balance and flexible knees try this. It will start you on your way to an erect, easy posture. Barefoot, line your body up, head, chest, and hips centered over the middle arch of your feet. Arms are straight in front of you at shoulder level, your weight is on your toes, your heels are lifted. Bend knees deeply and then gradually stand. Whoops! Try again.

The manner in which you sit and stand all the time
is important because the way you treat your body every
minute determines the shape you're in. Never stand
with your weight on one foot. Why do you girls do it?
Your body is thrown out of line; one shoulder and a
hip are raised, a thigh is enlarged. For the same reason
never sprawl while sitting. In your teens is the time to
lay the foundation for beautiful posture.

Of course there are girls and boys who are natural
athletes. They have compact, lithe muscles which move
with rhythmic grace, precision, and timing. There is
an easy smoothness in all their movements. Watch
the champions, they all have it; whether it's the execu-
tion of a swan dive or hitting a home run, the easy
smoothness is there. These people don't have to worry
about muscle co-ordination; they have it.

When Janet walks down the hall, you know from
her natural, easy grace and the rhythmic timing to her
walk that she is a "natural." It's true Janet has trained
for her swimming, but it's her inherent co-ordination
and zest which has put her at the top. Swimming on
your back is the best sport to improve your posture.

In walking, pull your body tall, chin level, abdomen
flat, rear tucked under, knees relaxed and slightly bent,
and feet pointing straight forward. Set your heel down
lightly, and give a slight push forward with the other
foot. Practice until you do it smoothly.

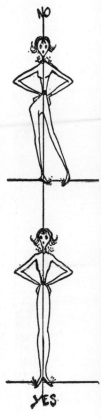

Ever watch the hurrying crowds in a bus station? The tense faces, heads thrust forward, hunched shoulders, and pounding heels are grim. Suitcases and packages banging into others with a kind of reckless, indifferent abandon, persons walking and turning abruptly, bumping into others create an off-key syncopation.

Take a deep breath, and pause. Not a redcap in sight? You pick up your suitcase and start away. Wait a minute; you dropped your glove. You aren't bending over stiff-legged, with your derrière high as a camel's hump! Instead you bend your knees with one foot slightly forward, keeping your head up and your back straight. Rising, push slightly with your back foot and lift yourself with your leg muscles. Do it in one smooth motion. Lift your suitcase in the same manner; the weight is taken with your leg muscles and not those of the back and shoulders. In carrying your case, walk erect, head up, and your carrying arm in a loose curve.

Why spoil this poised picture by diving headlong into a taxi as though you were clearing obstacles?

Here's the way. Face the front of the taxi and place the foot nearer the car inside, then slide into the seat and bring in the other foot.

When riding in a car let your feet rest comfortably flat on the floor, slide back on the seat, and rest your weight evenly on your sitting bones. With your head centered over the rib cage, you get the feeling of sitting tall, which is a very nice feeling to have.

At school choose a chair which lets your feet rest comfortably flat on the floor and again sit tall. In taking an exam sit relaxed, breathe a prayer, and know that you are doing your best.

In a beauty salon you see, under the driers, a row of women in the most awkward positions, with legs at grotesque angles. Seeing these ugly poses, you decide to sit gracefully—every time.

To know that you walk, sit, and stand with casual grace gives you a feeling of poise and self-assurance.

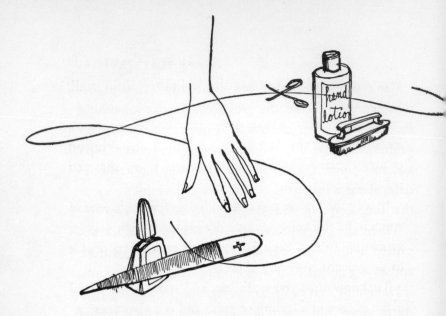

FINGER FLATTERY

Are your hands attractive or neglected? Perhaps the worst problem you can have is chewed nails, which are the result of nervous habits. But these difficulties and others are solved with intelligence.

There must be a reason back of nail chewing. Relax and think. When do you do it, and why? Is it in class, at home? Is it caused by nervousness or strain? When the reason is discovered, this ghastly habit is on the way to oblivion. Are you jittery because the blackboard blurs a little? Can you hear the teacher? With any such difficulties hasten to the school nurse for an eye-and-ear test or visit a doctor.

Can't you reason that you *must* stop? If your determination is feeble, the druggist will mix something for you that tastes as though it came from a witch's caldron. Frankly it is childish to be so dependent. Why not just stop? Look over the calendar for a special date, about a month hence, and be determined that at that time *you will have ten perfect nails. You can.*

There are other problem nails. Brittle nails are improved with a massage of warm oil. Drinking milk and eating gelatine do wonders for easily broken nails.

Hangnails can be a trial. Massage the cuticle with warm oil or cold cream, pushing back the cuticle only when it is soft and pliable. Never bite off hangnails; use the scissors. A manicure at regular intervals can prevent or at least improve this condition.

When starting your "salon" manicure lay all the articles on a towel before you. These are what you need: polish remover, cuticle remover, orange stick, cotton puff, emery board, colorless undercoat, polish, and paper tissues. Take your time and be thorough. Clean off all the old polish by saturating cotton with polish remover and pressing the cotton to the nail— pause a few seconds before rubbing toward the tip. For a neater manicure file your nails before soaking them. Always use an emery board, file toward the tip of the nail; shape the nails the way they look best (those long long nails are not for you if good taste is your guide). Wash your hands in warm sudsy water and put your nail brush into action. Push the cuticle back gently with the orange stick wrapped in cotton and saturated with cuticle remover. Wash again, dry thoroughly, using a towel to rub your nails briskly until they shine. Then brush on a colorless base coat and let it dry. For school the colorless or natural polish is appropriately smart.

I hear you exclaiming, "Those chem-lab stains ruin my hands and what that arts-and-crafts class does to my perfect manicure destroys my disposition." Remove the lab stains with a slice of lemon, the grime from arts-and-crafts with a good sudsing and a nail brush. Still streaked? Cup a little powdered pumice in the palm of your hand and scrub your hands gently. That does it; now rub in some hand lotion around the nails.

Well-kept hands must frame your well-groomed nails. Always dry your hands thoroughly, and in winter rub in cold cream or hand lotion, massaging any surplus on your elbows. When applying lotion or cream to your hands rub toward your wrists, imagining that you are smoothing on a pair of snug gloves.

Wear mittens or gloves when the snow drifts. Don't lose those mittens! Did you ever see the stacks of gloves and mittens in a "Lost & Found"? Rosabelle pinned her mittens with horse-blanket pins to the lining of her coat before she hung it away. Did you ever see a horse-blanket pin? It is an enormous safety pin similar to those made of gold which are sold as a smart accessory. Rosabelle started a trend and when twenty-three girls went to the hardware store to buy horse-blanket pins— imagine what happened.

What are you going to do with these well-groomed hands? The answer is to use your hands in a gracefully relaxed manner. Psychologists write pages to tell what hand gestures mean. They shower us with words, such as frustration, insecurity, inhibitions, and others longer and more impressive. The truth is this: *"Fidgety hands can't have glamor and charm."*

Can you guess what emotions these girls show? A "picker," picking at a scarf, an eyebrow? Or is she biting her pencil? A "patter," patting her hair on and on? Then there is the "desk or table tapper," a poor imitation of a woodpecker. When sitting hold your hands lightly in your lap, palms up, fingers relaxed, or have one hand in your lap and the other on a chair arm.

If your hands become tense and moist, squeeze them tightly into fists, then limp them completely by relaxing; squeeze and relax again. Stretch your fingers as far apart as possible, relax and repeat. When you are behind the scenes or alone, shake your hands until they become loose and floppy.

Well-groomed, relaxed hands give you a feeling of social ease—then forget yourself and think of others.

MORNING EXPRESS

What better time to start off with an air of casual perfection than in the morning? To be well groomed and alert at that time of day takes a bit of forethought. The requirements to smooth away this early-morning confusion are: a wide-awake feeling, after nine hours of sleep, and a routine to be practiced the night before.

No longer will it be a daily occurrence to go through your home imitating a miniature cyclone to find your notebook or your other shoe. You may take these hurricanes in stride, but your parents may wonder if rearing you is worth while. Surprise your family with your ability to cope and conquer by planning a systematic and efficient routine.

First, collect your books and put them near the door, along with your hat, gloves or mittens, scarf, and coat. Now is the time to give your clothes searching glances in order to forestall unpleasant surprises in the morning. Does your coat need more than a casual brush-off? Could the lining use a needle and thread? A light brushing prevents dust and soot from settling on your hat. Notice your glove seams because they have a diabolical habit of breaking at the most unexpected moments. When the weather man says "rain" or "snow," add your raincoat and galoshes.

Your morning's departure is now arranged except for your purse, which always needs a "daily in and out" because the interiors of purses are usually jungles of miscellaneous objects. Empty the bag; brush or sponge the lining. When dry, tuck in the essentials: fresh tissues, comb, handkerchief, correct change or bus ticket, money, and identification card.

Your "exit collection" is finished for early morning and the time has come to select the clothes to wear.

Cast a quick glance over them for any emergency: is the collar securely fastened to your sweater, the shoulder pads secure, and the hem stitched?

Neither can lingerie be taken for granted. Is the slip the correct length with tomorrow's skirt? Are there any wayward shoulder straps? Are all hooks and eyes sewed tightly?

Snags in hose and socks are a bother, but do look for them. Your best foot forward will be improved if your shoes have a daily polishing.

This is the time to find your costume jewelry, because of all the elusive objects to locate in the morning a bracelet or necklace is the most difficult.

Finally take a hint from the firemen; place your clothes from left to right in the order you will put them on. Now you are ready!

These suggestions will eliminate the time-consuming and patience-wearing scramble in the morning and will save your happy disposition. The family? They will be impressed—to put it mildly.

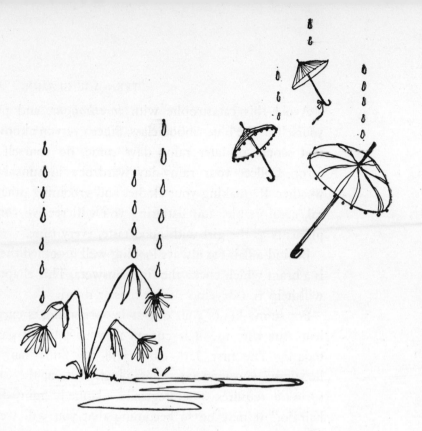

ANY OLD WAY ON A RAINY DAY?

Oh no, never! There is to be no drowsing on a rainy day. The alert girl arrives trim and poised.

When you haven't had your quota of nine hours' sleep, it's pleasantly easy to drift back to slumber. But if you do, what happens? Everything! You throw yourself together, your clothes are undecided whether to follow you to school, you eat no breakfast, you miss the bus and are tardy!

Avoid this catastrophe with *forethought,* and put yourself in the blue-ribbon class. Since everyone knows that sooner or later rainy days come, do yourself a favor. Collect your rainy-day wardrobe in sunshiny weather. By making your clothes and grooming practical, comfortable, and flattering you will receive compliments as the girl with good taste, every time.

Behind a flair for always looking well groomed there is a brain which clicks the right answers. This chapter will help you develop such a master mind.

For sunny hours your day-to-day grooming is excellent, but why the hair curlers in your public's gaze today? "The first dark cloud and my fluffy hair is hopeless," you may say. Hair which wilts at the first sprinkle requires a strategically planned "rainy-day hair-do." It may be so becoming that you will wear it every day. It has happened.

Stray locks can be held in place with a wide band of ribbon across the top of your head and fastened under the hair in the back. For slightly wavy hair cut long a neat page boy may be the answer. Anna Belle, at the first sign of rainy weather, wears her hair brushed sleekly up and fastened in a little curl right on top of her head. She adds a small ribbon bow, and on her it is something special. With hair truly straight why not wear braids which could be looped, wound over the ears, pinned across the back or on top? Hair

too thin for braids? Plait in some bright ribbons—
what could be more fetching on a blue Monday? If
the dampness makes little curls around your face a
lucky star is on your shoulder.

A moan, a groan! Splashed socks! Your appearance
and poise are ruined. This catastrophe is overcome by
improving the way you walk. Swing your legs from
the thigh joints and point your feet straight ahead.
Walk lightly and don't drag your heels. Remember
about walking in the chapter, "Here's a Wish"?

When walking down the street on a dismal day,
wouldn't you like a rainbow round your shoulders?

A gay plaid umbrella is the answer. Take a hint
from the French, who judge an umbrella by the color
it reflects on your face. A rosy glow becoming? Select
reds in solid colors or plaids, predominantly red.
Purple shadows? They are not for you.

Ruffled umbrellas can be a deft feminine wile, but
when ruffles are even slightly tired, there is nothing
droopier. For practicality ruffled umbrellas are shunned.
Carry umbrellas of light gay colors for a rainy summer
season. A pretty one is turquoise with white polka
dots, and there are the chintz kind with wonderfully
colored flowers. Such umbrellas give a lighthearted
lift to any summer shower.

By all means harmonize the colors of your umbrella
and raincoat or the result may be a clashing of colors.

Practicality and glamor are combined by Mildred, a petite black-haired charmer who wears a brilliant yellow slicker which has well-cut inverted pleats down the back to give her height and an action-free fit with no bulkiness. Her umbrella is yellow plastic. Mildred's sparkling eyes, dazzling smile, and a raindrop on her nose, all framed with her yellow hood, make a pretty picture on any rainy day. Brown-eyed Marilyn is smart in a vivid plaid coat. Plaids are gay and add zest to your life, but not for a completely over-all picture. With her plaid coat Marilyn keeps her umbrella and other accessories solid colors. Do you remember the discussion about solid colors and plaids in the chapter "Precious Little"?

There are dozens of colors and styles of raincoats because of the different climate in various parts of the country. If the rain in your locality is penetratingly chilly, you will want a snug, warm coat, probably the cravenetted kind. In warm localities the light trans-

parent capes are often worn. A crowded school bus is
no place for a cape. When you are sitting, the corner
of a cape drags on the floor and, wham! Someone's
foot steps through the dragging cape.

For a unified effect purses and galoshes are part of
the over-all picture. You say, "Old shoes instead of
galoshes." Of course not! Sit in class with wet shoes?
Chilling and sneezing may be your rewards!

A damp, soggy purse ruins the best-laid plans. That's
another reason plastic handbags are the favorite with
the school crowd. An inexpensive plastic envelope
with a zipper wins enthusiastic approval as a rainy-
day accessory.

Rainy weather means wet gloves and mittens, which
dry quicker when they are hung on a hook or pinned
to your coat. Never stuff damp gloves in your pockets.

Create your own plans for rainy days. The weather
may be a discouraging mess, but you will be the opposite, a beautiful contrast. Who said a dreary day?

MEND YOUR WAYS

Isn't it slightly stupid to be a "Sloppy Sue" because your clothes were left on the closet floor? The most expensive or the best-made clothes in the world can't take such carelessness, and it isn't smart.

To have and to keep clothes in perfect condition takes a technique with a system, and the results are worth every minute you spend. If you think that you were born to be careless, there are two choices: first, think over the situation and develop your own particular system. This is the sensible approach, and you will be a "Smooth Sue," always groomed and always ready. The second choice is to be plain lazy: this brings hurt feelings, tears, and tantrums, because the gang isn't going to wait while you search for your bathing suit or change a soiled collar on your favorite sweater. You'll miss a lot of fun, and you should if you are that indifferent.

You are decided—whining isn't for you. A specialized technique it will be; so—on your way!

A clean closet with all the articles placed in an orderly fashion is necessary. You who have a large airy closet of your own are fortunate; some of you haven't any. If that is your problem, ask for some corner of the room, fasten folding screens on each side, fit shelves across, and place a rod for hangers; or get an unpainted cupboard, with clothes rods, which can be bought reasonably.

Make the closet very personally yours. Is pale green a favorite color? Paint the walls green and paste cutout roses here and there. Or with a lavish hand scatter silver stars hither and yon on blue walls. Is sailing your hobby? Sailboats skimming over the blue and an anchor over the door show your ingenuity. Tie a ribbon around the necks of your empty perfume bottles and hang them from the clothes rod—when the door is opened—hmm nice!

Busy girls need timesaving devices, and for this reason cellophane clothes and shoe bags, along with clear plastic hat boxes, are convenient necessities. An-

other stratagem is to put articles together which are
to be used on the same occasion, such as galoshes, umbrellas, and raincoats.

Your bureau drawers a mess? Take courage and
mend your ways. The various articles are neatly separated with transparent plastic envelopes or boxes.
Another good idea is an office cabinet, one of those
metal affairs with many shallow drawers: one to hold
sweaters, another for bras, another for panties, etc.
Order is very easy with these shallow drawers.

The insides of bureau drawers are often painted
(there is a perfumed lacquer on the market for this
very purpose) or lined with gift-wrapping paper.
Dolores lined her bureau drawers with foil paper in
her favorite colors.

Everything is ready for your clothes.

After wearing your dresses, suits, and sweaters brush
and hang them where the fresh breezes blow through
them. Slips, bras, and panties are washed *every* day;
and in warm weather, if you wear a girdle, add it to
the bowl of suds. In wintertime, with grime and soot
floating through the air, your clothes are soaked in
soapy warm water a few minutes; rinse, squeeze, and
hang with care. After a girdle is washed, roll it in a
towel and pat out the excess water; hang it where
warm air circulates. Never dry a girdle hastily by
placing it on a radiator!

Sweaters are your treasures, so warm, so light, so fluffy in their jewel colors. Treat them with loving care. The first step in washing a wool sweater is to draw an outline of it on a piece of wrapping-paper. This is your pattern when you are patting the washed sweater back to its original size and shape. If you have several sweaters, a drying frame is handy, but don't forget to adjust the frame to the correct size of your sweater. Frames aren't necessary for Dacron and Orlon sweaters because sweaters of synthetic fibers retain their shape.

With mild soap flakes thoroughly dissolved in luke-warm water whip up a deep suds. Remove any buttons which might fade or tear the fabric, turn the sweater inside out, and wash under water gently; *don't rub*. Let the suds come through the material, holding it with your hands cupped.

When lifting the sweater use both hands and lift in a mass. Two sudsings may be necessary.

Rinse and rinse in lukewarm water, let the clear water ooze through, still cupping the sweater in your hands. Squeeze out the water and spread the sweater flat on a towel, roll, and gently press out the excess moisture.

Put a wool sweater on a dry towel, cover with your cutout paper "pattern," pat, and pin the sweater in place to dry. All sweaters are kept away from any heat.

When the sweater is almost dry, iron it on the wrong side with a slightly warm iron and a pressing cloth. Don't drag the iron—lift it from place to place. The pressing cloth will leave a little moisture, so cover the sweater with some wrapping paper and iron over the paper until it's dry. Fold the dry sweater lightly and lay it flat; never put sweaters on hangers.

Mittens and wool socks are washed in the same way —always use lukewarm suds, and never rub. The washing directions which come with gloves are written by experts; by following the directions your gloves last longer and look better. Leather gloves are washed and rinsed on the hands. When a little soap is added to the last rinse water, the leather is more pliable.

Of course some clothes need dry cleaning, but money is saved by keeping all your clothes brushed, aired, and the spots removed. Pressing is no problem with a pressing cloth and a steam iron. Wool skirts won't be shiny when the pressing cloth is removed before it is ironed dry. Wool, silk, and rayon are pressed on the right side with the pressing cloth between material and the iron. Velvets and corduroys need steam from your bathroom shower or the teakettle. Felt hats are revived when they are brushed counterclockwise before a steaming teakettle.

In skipping from hats to heels, how are yours? How often do *you* look at them? Other people do. Keep your shoes in excellent condition with heel straightening, polishing, and cleaning. Use shoe trees to help your shoes keep their shape.

All these tasks take time; therefore acquire all the timesaving equipment you possibly can.

First of all, save your pennies and buy a steam iron. With it your pressing is done quickly and easily. The following aids are helpful:

> well-padded ironing board
> pressing cloth
> drying frames for socks and sweaters
> mending basket with many needles
> clear plastic boxes and envelopes
> stiff whisk broom
> soft hatbrush

The secret of that clean, fresh, well-cared-for look is to give your clothes daily care, because good grooming is a continuous, everyday process.

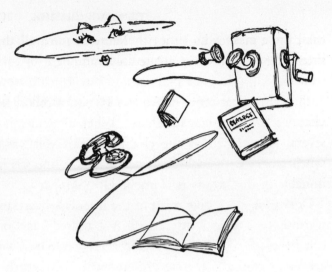

TALK OF THE TOWN

Let's make any conversation sweet and low, with a voice as attractive as your appearance. Usually voices are underestimated and undervalued treasures. By developing the possibilities of your voice you heighten your charm and increase the assurance of your poise. Does your voice sound friendly or does it strike clashing sparks? Listen to voices. They are: harried or happy, jittery or serene, demure or belligerent, exultant or depressed, indifferent or eager. A dynamic voice can calm a mob or incite a riot. Many of you are baby-sitters. Does your voice create an atmosphere of calm security?

The crisp, clear tones of Audrey Hepburn reflect her vitality and blithe, vibrant charm. When an actor plays several roles, listen to the changes in his voice as it synchronizes with each character. Alec Guinness is in-imitable in this art, as is Cornelia Otis Skinner.

Does your voice give a lift to the listener's heart and warmth to a casual utterance? A hundred reactions can be received from the same sentence. Say, "You are late," teasingly, worriedly, annoyedly, coquettishly, hopefully, fearfully, dejectedly, amazedly, spitefully, angrily. The ability to reflect your passing moods by the inflection of your voice is exciting fun or potentially dangerous. What will your voice express?

A whiner? You know the pessimist. Nothing was, is, or ever will be fair and square in this world to the whiner. The public could happily dispense with this pessimistic dim-wit.

An insistently nagging voice makes everyone grit his teeth. Essential? Don't you believe it. Ninety-nine per cent of the nagging can be eliminated with intelli-gence.

What else does your voice tell? Perhaps it doesn't tell, perhaps it's a mumble; many persons speak with-out moving their lips. Edgar Bergen and the villain of

a spy thriller speak distinctly without apparently moving their facial muscles, but you aren't trained to do
it and are merely irritatingly indistinct. It's laziness and
ignorance. An effective exercise to increase the needed
flexibility of tongue and lips is to say the consonants
rapidly, over and over again, thus:

> Bub bub bub bub bub
> dud dud dud dud dud
> fuf fuf fuf fuf fuf
> lul lul lul lul lul

Your enunciation is clear and crisp? Listen to Lowell
Thomas.

Monotonous voices, dull and colorless, are avoided
by all public speakers. A trial lawyer is a master of
the dramatic pause, the timing, and change of pitch.
You may not attend a trial, but all of you can hear the
voices of top-flight radio announcers, all of whom have
distinct, well-modulated voices with a warm sponta-
neity to give them expression. There is the calm as-
sured voice of Edward R. Murrow and the superb
diction of Orson Welles. Listen and compare, because
the best-trained speakers in the world are heard with
the turn of a radio knob.

"How can I improve?" Raise and lower your voice
every few phrases. Sing *A-a-a-a-a-a-ah,* starting in the
lowest register, and ending in the highest. Hum until

you feel it in your nose and cheeks. This is the answer to a flat monotonous voice.

"At school, I hear my voice go dead level or higher when I recite. I can't talk in class," you moan. Relax! Everyone sometime has had that unnerving experience. It is tension. A good big yawn will relax your throat, face, and tongue. You are in the front row? By taking a deep breath and by knowing your lesson thoroughly you can relax and talk easily.

When doing homework Mary often writes the answers, but answers written or not, she always says them aloud, which is a check on the pronunciation of difficult words. In class Mary's answers have organization and assurance. She carries this technique into her debating club, where a congressman said that he would give a thousand dollars if he could cross a stage and start to speak as naturally as Mary does. A smart girl who believes in forethought.

With a voice fresh, clear, crisp, sparkling, or smooth

you certainly can't have a dull and dreary conversation. Don't wail, "I never know what to say." Frankly that is more easily remedied than if you were a "chitter-chatterer."

Knowledge is the basis of conversation. The more you know the wider are your interests and the more varied is your information. How many persons have an intellectual curiosity? Very few! My father was the most interesting conversationalist I have known. His interests were many and his knowledge profound. Busy as he was, he learned something new every day. Why don't you start acquiring knowledge in those idle minutes scattered through the day?

No time for newspapers? Who *can* read every word? But here is a technique which hurries an understanding eye. Read the headlines and the first two paragraphs of a story; here is the action, climax, and the essential material; the copyeditor sees that every headline, every story, is streamlined with terse, pertinent facts. For a week read the sports page, and you are an appreciative audience for your brother's comments on the last game, and what is more important, he enjoys talking to you.

A newspaper tells what is going to happen next, the games, concerts, release of stamps and records, exhibits, sports events, and movies. Be the girl who sees it first— in the newspaper.

Reading is one of the quickest ways to acquire information. When you have a teacher who has a discriminating mind and a keen appreciation of the best literature, listen to her every word. She is lighting the paths of greatness for you. You simply can't read great books and stay the same. Books push out your horizons, increase your knowledge, and give you a more sympathetic understanding of others. The books of the world's brilliant, penetrating, and compassionate minds are as near as your public library.

The greatest book of all is the Bible. Oh no, it isn't dull. More people read the Bible than any other book because it offers a powerful faith based on unselfish love and eternal compassion. Is there anything to equal, "If thou canst believe, all things are possible to him that believeth." (Mark 9:23.)

If you are a beginner, read the Book of Esther and imagine you are there in a luxurious hall surrounded by a proud and arrogant court. Esther, a young and beautiful queen, stands with treachery and death on each side of her. Counseled to conceal her Jewish origin from her headstrong husband, she touches her crown and jeweled scepter, and looks steadily at this man who is her husband and her king. Esther proudly and defiantly implores, "How can I endure to see the evil which has come upon my kindred, for I, too, am a Jew. Repudiate your royal decree to

slay the Jews. Let my people live." Think of the electri-
fying words. A girl's intense loyalty made a powerful
king recall his words. Of course you admire loyalty.
Give it abundantly to your school, your friends, and
most of all to your family.

Mark, who wrote another book of the Bible, was
about your age, seventeen, when he first became interested in Jesus. Mark, with his sincerity and his earnest-
ness, had a consuming curiosity to know about this
man called the Messiah. Following and watching from
the edge of the crowd, Mark stayed in the background.
The day of the Crucifixion he was there, still wonder-
ing, still questioning. Turning to go, he brushed against
a man who was leaning on the Cross. A tough, battle-
hardened soldier, with weary eyes above a stubble of
beard, muttered, "Truly he was the Son of God." This
was the turning point of Mark's life. The Bible has
changed the course of many lives. The Bible gives you
these: a faith to live by, an understanding of human
nature, and a code of conduct. No other book gives
so much.

The tragedy of grief, the nobility of unselfish love,
and the loyalty of faith in the Bible are echoed in the
magnificent underlying rhythms of great music. Symphonic music with sweeping movements building to a
superb climax must be heard. Your record collection
needs a Beethoven symphony, start with his fifth or

sixth, and one of Brahms, perhaps his fourth in E Minor. If you are already an avid collector of symphonic music, include some records by Benny Goodman and David Brubeck. Other people enjoy the expressive music of Verdi's *Rigoletto*. A part of you belongs to music and to art.

You shun modern art? Picasso puzzles you completely! Keep an open mind. After a few exhibits the color, the line, or the mood will exert an appeal. The best of modern art is vigorously creative.

Every city has photography exhibits to be visited. Study the composition, the balance of light and shadow. Do you like it? Would you change the picture in any way?

When people discover that you know something, no matter how little, about a subject, they are delighted to tell you more; people long for an interested audience. You will fit into many groups regardless of any differences in age. Your circle of friends and acquaintances becomes larger. And your shyness drops away. Conversation? You will have the spark to start a thousand! After a conversation is started, do become interested in what other people say; be an intelligent and enthusiastic listener. Be careful that you never monopolize the conversation, never brag, and never pry into personal affairs. An open mind is best on controversial topics.

Fill your mind with interesting information so that there is neither time nor inclination for cattiness and petty gossip. Spite exposes the condition of your heart. The public recognizes your inferiority and your determination to destroy the one you envy. Bite your tongue, clench your hands, leave, but don't repeat that bit of hateful gossip. How would you feel if you heard a group tearing you apart? Don't do it to others. An innocent act or remark is embroidered with jealousy and malice until it is horrible. A human failing is to add a dramatic bit which provides a moment in the limelight at the expense of someone else. Those who emphasize their gossip by saying, "I know for a fact . . ." invariably close their minds to the truth. No one really likes a gossip. There are always questions in the back of the listener's mind: Why is she doing this? Will she ever do it to me? She probably will. Hatred is the reward of a gossip. "She never says a mean thing about anyone," is a valuable recommendation for a friend or for a job.

For a career of any kind this book helps you with your future as well as now. Being perfectly groomed and attractively dressed, you have poise and assurance; to these you add the sparkle, the warmth and friendliness for others. The result is a charming person. YOU.

CHRISTMAS SYMPHONY

Snowflakes floating, cold stars twinkling in the crisp air. Christmas is zest, excitement, gifts, and parties. Let your dreams and your happiness soar to the farthest star. The fun and the laughter, the gleam of candle-light, and the scent of evergreens are forever yours. Always you will remember the reverent telling of the Christmas story.

You tingle with anticipation, it's wonderful to be alive. What to do! What to give! Stars in your eyes and your feet flying.

For a holiday wonderland, plan with forethought. Unless you are of Quiz Kid caliber, let lists take the harried look out of your eyes (your disposition, too) and put in the "everything's taken care of" gleam. It's worth the planning.

There's a plan—which takes a master mind to sched-ule; the money goes here, it must go there, and Time has only sixty busy minutes for every hour.

The presents are first and are chosen with thought-ful discrimination and appreciation of the other per-son's desires. If time is passing and you are having a bout with the flu, why not give magazine subscrip-

tions? Your man of the hour might prefer the *National Geographic* twelve times a year. There's usually some-one in the neighborhood who takes subscriptions, and all department stores do. Gifts with imagination and taste are more fun and are remembered far longer.

For gifts to be wrapped why not be the girl who does it with flair? "My dear, she does it divinely," will be echoed again and again. If it becomes your hobby, you will be collecting unusual items all year. Foil paper is effective but expensive; used strategically (with no waste), it goes far. There's the ribbon which comes around boxes all through the year, and the five-and-dime abounds in decorative accessories; the evergreen by your front door or a spray of cedar from the grocer will furnish you with sprigs of green. Here is an ade-quate list with which to start:

> wrapping paper, various colors in the foil, suède, fluorescent finishes, and white tissue
> sprigs of cedar and tiny cones

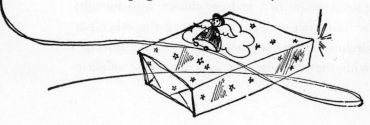

small jar of white poster paint
artificial flowers and leaves
bottle of metallic glitter and box of artificial
snow
gummed stars, all colors and sizes
Christmas-tree decorations, tiny bells, remnants
of ribbon
Scotch Tape

Wrap a small package in silver paper, and with Scotch Tape fasten on top a tiny red house and ever-green trees from a toyshop. The roof and the edges of these small trees are painted with the white poster paint, and while it is wet, sprinkled with silvery glitter particles.

Another package is wrapped in sky-blue, shiny paper dotted with minute silver stars. A little pink cloud (formerly an envelope lining) is cut and pasted on. Poise a miniature gold angel securely on the cloud. Shall I tell you about one more? Wrap this box in either blue-violet or deep purple paper, and anchor to the top an enormous rosette of bright pink tulle tied with a narrow silver ribbon. These packages fairly sing of the holidays. Why not try and see what unusually lovely packages you can create. If you enjoy doing this, you may become a consultant of gift wrapping for a large paper firm, traveling, talking, and demonstrating to various groups.

There are gifts which can't be wrapped in paper, the gifts which are part of your shining hours of thoughtfulness. Running errands for a sick neighbor, taking the junior editions to their rehearsals for the Christmas play, giving the living room a perpetual neat-as-a-pin routine. Yes, I know you are doing more than three persons now; so is Mother; do something special for her. Presents gifted by your heart envelop you with a glow of happiness and you—why you are a Christmas angel.

The gifts are under wraps and the inventory of your clothes for the big blasts and little popovers is on. It takes a great deal of concentration and thinking for yourself so there are no harum-scarum decisions. Your lists of things to change or make, anything to mend, and what to buy. The primaries get the top of the list.

You say dancing shoes are your major primary. Buy those which harmonize with the majority of your clothes. Gold, silver, and crimson colors are the most versatile, and kid leathers take more wearing than satin or brocade. If your ankles are among your best features you can wear the more decorative and the more daring. Every girl, sometime, has a yen for jeweled heels.

"And dresses," you moan, "every dress is worn." Too wilted after the Thanksgiving whirl? The easiest thing in the world is to make one evening dress from two which have had their fling. I know three girls who made their holiday money by renovating such dresses for others. Janet, who has a strong feeling for flattering line, designed and helped to fit; the others cut, sewed, and finished. The results are spectacular; why not, with three clever brains?

Some of you girls maintain that a sheath dress is the answer to every problem if your figure has grace. Ellis, with her fabulous imagination and creative ability, has a white crepe sheath dress which she calls her "million-dollar change-over." Her accessories are: a white tulle overskirt of cascading ruffles, a billowing net skirt ex-

travagantly sequin-sprinkled, a royal blue crushed cummerbund, a stole which makes a blazing scarlet sweep from the shoulders to the floor, a short emerald-green satin bolero, a flirtatious taffeta apron, and a provocative lace cape. Ellis danced the happy holidays through in one dress which could be demure, dramatic, or dreamy, but always devastating. It's only adding imagination to a basic dress. There are other ideas for evening dresses in the chapter "Unite and Divide."

All beautiful colors are Christmas colors, and against their swirling motion many times, by wearing a perfect white dress, you are the evening's sensation.

The breath-taking kaleidoscope of Christmas-tree decorations, the scent of pine needles, the fragrance of flowers and perfume, the glow of candlelight, and an aura of happiness whisper a memorable melody for your Christmas symphony.

FINALE

Aren't you happily amazed with your accomplishments of perfect grooming, pleasant voice, and graceful carriage, all enhanced with flattering clothes? Your new knowledge of the wizardry of color and line gives a flair and style to your individuality. With these attributes an integrated part of your life, you now have the self-confidence which lets you forget yourself and become interested in others. True beauty is kindness, generosity, cheerfulness, and gentleness which gives a glow to your face and charm to your manner. Your improved appearance and new capabilities impress and delight your family, capture masculine hearts, and captivate your friends.

INDEX